THE SOUL'S JOURNEY THROUGH THE ZODIAC

SIGNS, HOUSES, AND THE EVOLUTION OF CONSCIOUSNESS

Tina Ketch

THE SOUL'S JOURNEY THROUGH THE ZODIAC
SINGS, HOUSES, AND THE EVOLUTION OF CONSCIOUSNESS

This book is intended for educational, inspirational, and informational purposes only. The ideas and perspectives shared within these pages reflect the author's personal research, experiences, and interpretations of astrology and spiritual development. Readers are encouraged to explore these insights thoughtfully and apply them according to their own discernment.

The author and publisher make no guarantees regarding personal outcomes based on the material presented in this book.

ISBN: 979-8-9951587-5-2
eISBN: 979-8-9951587-6-9

For information, inquiries, or permissions, contact:
https://TinaKetch.com
TinaKetch@me.com
https://YouTube.com/TinaKetch

PREFACE

Since the earliest days of civilization, humanity has lifted its eyes toward the heavens with wonder. The night sky carries a quiet reminder that our lives unfold inside a much greater story, one shaped by cycles, seasons, and unseen rhythms that move through all things.

My own curiosity about these cosmic patterns began during a season of deep searching. I found myself drawn into the study of spiritual traditions, religion, and astrology, not to escape life, but to understand it. Over time, I discovered that the zodiac is not merely a collection of personality traits; it is a symbolic map of the soul's evolution.

As I studied the twelve signs, I began to see them as stages of growth that live within every human life. Each sign carries a lesson, courage, stability, curiosity, belonging, creativity, refinement, balance, transformation, truth, mastery, vision, and spiritual compassion. Together they form a complete journey: the soul learning how to become itself fully, and then how to return to wholeness.

This book is written for readers who sense that their lives have meaning beyond the surface, and who want language for the inner changes they have lived through. You do not need to be an astrologer to read these pages. You only need a willingness to reflect, to recognize patterns, and to meet yourself with honesty.

We may enter life under one sign, but the journey of the soul moves through them all. As you read, you may recognize certain chapters as mirrors of what you are living now, while others illuminate what you have already mastered, or what may be calling you forward.

My hope is that these reflections help you trust your timing, honor your growth, and see your experiences as purposeful, even when the path is not easy to understand. The stars above do not control your destiny, but they can remind you of something powerful: you are part of a living universe, and your life is a sacred unfolding.

TABLE OF CONTENTS

INTRODUCTION

The Zodiac as a Map of the Soul

The zodiac has long been studied as a language of symbols, one that reflects the rhythms of human life through the movement of the heavens. Yet beyond prediction and personality, the zodiac can be understood as something even more intimate: a map of the soul's unfolding.

Most people first meet the zodiac as a set of traits connected to birth dates. But in its deeper form, the zodiac describes a living cycle of consciousness, twelve archetypal stages the soul moves through as it grows, learns, loves, and transforms. Each sign represents a stage of human development. Together they form a complete circle, reflecting the journey of the soul as it grows, struggles, awakens, and ultimately returns to a deeper understanding of unity and love.

How this book is organized

Part I explores the twelve zodiac signs as stages of soul development. Part II moves into the twelve houses, the life areas where these lessons unfold. Part III brings the map together by showing how signs, houses, planets, aspects, and the birth chart work as an integrated language. Part IV focuses on integration: awakening, embodiment, and living your soul map with intention.

Every human life contains these twelve lessons. We may be born under one sign, but the journey of life invites us to experience them all. At different times, we embody the courage of Aries, the patience of Taurus, the curiosity of Gemini, or the deep transformation of Scorpio. The zodiac is, therefore, not simply something we are; it is something we move through.

How to use this book

You can read straight through, or you can move intuitively, returning to the sign or theme that reflects what you are living now. After each chapter, pause with the Reflection prompts. Let them become a mirror, helping you translate insight into lived awareness.

In this way, the zodiac becomes a profound teacher. It reminds us that life is not random. Our experiences, challenges, relationships, and discoveries are part of a larger unfolding. Each phase of life offers a new opportunity for growth and understanding.

When we begin to see the zodiac as a pathway rather than a label, a remarkable shift occurs. We recognize that every sign holds wisdom for us, and that the journey through these twelve energies is guiding us toward a fuller expression of our true selves.

And when we learn to listen to their symbolic language, we discover that the journey of the zodiac is also a journey inward, toward greater consciousness, compassion, and wholeness.

PART I:

THE ZODIAC,

TWELVE ARCHETYPES OF THE SOUL

CHAPTER 1:
ARIES, THE BIRTH OF THE SELF

THE SYMBOL OF ARIES ♈

The symbol of Aries resembles the curved horns of a ram rising upward from a central point. This simple glyph carries profound symbolic meaning. The two sweeping curves suggest motion, emergence, and the first stirring of life pushing forward into the world.

In symbolic language, the Aries glyph can be seen as the moment when energy bursts forth from a single origin point. It resembles a seed breaking open in the soil or the first rays of sunlight appearing above the horizon at dawn.

Aries is the beginning of the zodiac cycle, and its symbol reflects that sacred moment when life moves from potential into action.

The ram itself embodies determination, strength, and fearless movement. Rams climb steep mountains and move forward even when the path is difficult. In the same way, Aries energy encourages the soul to move forward with courage and initiative.

Ancient Origins of Aries

The story of Aries reaches back thousands of years to the earliest civilizations that studied the heavens.

Ancient astronomers in Mesopotamia and Babylon observed that the Sun entered the constellation we now call Aries at the beginning of spring. This moment corresponded with the vernal equinox, when day and night are equal, and the earth begins to awaken from the stillness of winter.

For ancient cultures, this time of year symbolized renewal and rebirth. Crops began to grow, animals gave birth, and the earth seemed to breathe again.

Because of this powerful seasonal symbolism, Aries became associated with the beginning of life itself.

The ram was chosen as the sign's emblem because it represented vitality, leadership, and strength within the natural world. Rams often lead their flocks and move forward with determination, qualities that perfectly reflect the pioneering spirit of Aries.

Over time, astrologers recognized Aries as the first step in the zodiacal cycle, the moment when life begins its journey through the twelve stages of growth and experience.

Aries in Mythology

One of the most famous myths connected to Aries comes from ancient Greece and tells the story of the Golden Ram.

According to legend, the ram was sent by the gods to rescue two children, Phrixus and Helle, who were in danger. The ram carried them across the sky to safety, demonstrating courage and divine protection.

After reaching safety, the ram's golden fleece became a sacred treasure. It was later sought by the hero Jason and the Argonauts in their legendary quest.

This myth reflects many of the qualities associated with Aries, bravery, adventure, and the willingness to embark on a heroic journey.

The ram's golden fleece became a symbol of achievement and divine favor, reminding us that bold action often leads to profound rewards.

The Beginning of the Zodiac Journey

Every great story begins with a moment of awakening.

In the zodiac, that awakening begins with Aries.

Aries represents the stage where consciousness first recognizes itself as an individual presence. The soul moves from unity with the greater whole into the experience of being a distinct being capable of action, choice, and exploration.

This realization is the foundation of all growth.

Before the soul can learn love, wisdom, patience, or compassion, it must first discover its own identity.

Aries is the moment when the soul says:

“I am.”

The Spark of Life

Imagine the moment when a flame is first lit. A small spark appears, delicate yet powerful, capable of growing into a great fire.

Aries carries this same energy.

It is the force that says:

Step forward.
Take the first breath.
Begin the journey.

This awakening is not quiet or passive. Aries energy is bold, direct, and full of vitality. It pushes forward with enthusiasm and courage, eager to experience life in all its forms.

Like a newborn child opening its eyes to the world, the Aries stage of the soul is filled with curiosity and instinctive determination.

Courage and Initiative

Aries teaches the soul one of the most essential lessons of life:

the courage to begin.

Every meaningful achievement begins with a first step. Yet taking that step often requires bravery, because the outcome is rarely certain.

The Aries spirit encourages us to move forward even when we do not yet see the entire path.

It is the energy behind:

- starting a new career
- pursuing a dream
- beginning a creative project
- standing up for one's beliefs

Without Aries energy, progress would never occur. Life would remain static and unmoving.

Aries reminds us that growth requires action.

Aries and the Energy of Youth

In the arc of human development, Aries reflects the earliest stage of life.

We see its influence in young children who explore the world with fearless curiosity. A child's first steps, first words, and first declarations of independence all carry the spirit of Aries.

Children rarely hesitate when trying something new. They fall, stand up again, and continue exploring.

This persistence reflects the natural vitality of Aries energy.

Although adulthood often introduces caution and hesitation, the Aries flame never disappears completely. It remains within us as the inner voice that encourages us to begin again whenever life offers a new opportunity.

The Shadow of Aries

Every zodiac sign carries both light and shadow.

When Aries energy becomes unbalanced, its strengths can turn into challenges. Courage may become recklessness. Confidence may become arrogance. Initiative may become impatient.

Because Aries moves quickly and instinctively, it may act before considering the consequences or the perspectives of others.

Yet these challenges are not failures; they are part of the learning process.

Through experience, the Aries spirit gradually learns to temper action with awareness and wisdom.

The lesson is not to extinguish the fire of Aries but to guide it wisely.

Fire, when directed with care, becomes a powerful source of warmth, creativity, and transformation.

The Gift of Aries

The greatest gift of Aries is the awakening of personal power.

It teaches the soul that it has the ability to act, to create, and to shape its own experiences.

This realization forms the foundation of the entire zodiac journey.

Aries reminds us that life is not something that merely happens to us. It is something we participate in actively.

When Aries energy is balanced and conscious, it gives us the strength to pursue our dreams, to stand up for what we believe in, and to begin new chapters with confidence.

Reflection

Take a moment to consider the moments in your life when you felt called to begin something new.

When did you feel the spark of courage urging you forward?

Perhaps it was the start of a relationship, a creative endeavor, a spiritual awakening, or a life-changing decision.

In each of those moments, the energy of Aries was present.

Within every person lives this same courageous spirit.

The question is not whether the Aries energy exists within us; it does.

The question is whether we allow its flame to guide us toward growth and discovery.

The Journey Continues

Aries begins the great cycle of the zodiac, but it is only the first step.

Once the soul awakens to individuality, it must learn how to sustain and nurture life. It must discover stability, value, and connection with the physical world.

These lessons await in the next stage of the zodiac journey.

The soul, having taken its first courageous step into existence, now turns toward the grounding energy of Taurus, where the roots of life begin to take form.

CHAPTER 2:
TAURUS, THE ROOTS OF LIFE

THE SYMBOL OF TAURUS ♉

The symbol of Taurus resembles the head and horns of a bull rising from a circle. The circle represents wholeness, matter, and the physical world, while the horns suggest power, strength, and stability.

Unlike the upward surge of Aries, the Taurus symbol appears grounded and steady. It conveys the idea of a solid foundation and enduring strength.

The bull has long been associated with fertility, abundance, and the life-giving power of the earth. Ancient cultures revered the bull as a sacred animal because it symbolized the energy that nourishes life and sustains growth.

The Taurus glyph reminds us that after the initial spark of life, the next step is to root that life in stability and nourishment.

Ancient Origins of Taurus

Taurus is one of the oldest constellations known to humanity. Its presence in the night sky has been recognized for more than five thousand years, appearing in the star charts of ancient Babylonian, Egyptian, and Mesopotamian civilizations.

In many ancient cultures, Taurus was associated with the fertility of the earth and the abundance of nature. The arrival of the Sun into the region of Taurus coincided with the season when crops began to flourish and the land revealed its richness.

For agricultural societies, this period was sacred. The earth was awakening, and the promise of nourishment and survival was renewed.

Because of this connection with nature's abundance, Taurus became a symbol of fertility, prosperity, and the sustaining power of the material world.

The ancients understood something profound: life does not flourish through inspiration alone. It requires stability, nourishment, and care.

Taurus in Mythology

In mythology, Taurus is often associated with the story of Zeus transforming himself into a magnificent white bull.

According to the myth, Zeus took the form of a gentle and beautiful bull to approach the princess Europa. Entranced by the creature's calm presence, Europa climbed onto its back. The bull then carried her across the sea to a distant land where a new destiny awaited her.

This myth reflects the quiet yet powerful nature of Taurus energy. Unlike the fiery impulsiveness of Aries, Taurus moves with patience and steadiness. Its power lies not in sudden action but in endurance and reliability.

The bull in mythology often represents the sacred connection between humanity and the earth, reminding us that stability and abundance arise when we live in harmony with the natural world.

The Second Step of the Soul's Journey

After the soul awakens to individuality in Aries, it enters the next stage of evolution: learning how to live within the physical world.

This is the domain of Taurus.

While Aries declares "I am," Taurus follows with the realization:

"I have."

The soul begins to understand the importance of resources, security, and the ability to sustain life. It learns to value the body, the earth, and the physical environment in which it exists.

This stage of the journey teaches the soul how to build a stable foundation.

Without this grounding, the spark of Aries would burn out quickly. Taurus provides the steady fuel that allows life to continue growing.

The Earth Element

Taurus is the first earth sign of the zodiac, and the element of earth symbolizes solidity, reliability, and connection with the material world.

Earth energy teaches patience.

Seeds planted in the soil do not grow instantly. They require time, nourishment, and care. Taurus embodies this slow and steady rhythm of nature.

The soul learns that true growth often unfolds gradually.

In a world that sometimes values speed and immediacy, Taurus reminds us that the most enduring achievements are built through persistence and dedication.

The Power of Stability

One of Taurus's greatest gifts is the ability to create stability.

The soul, having awakened in Aries, must now learn to build something lasting. This may take the form of physical resources, emotional security, or a sense of belonging in the world.

Taurus energy teaches the importance of:

- patience
- reliability

- consistency
- perseverance

These qualities allow the soul to create structures that support growth and well-being.

Without stability, life becomes chaotic and uncertain. Taurus provides the steady ground upon which dreams can take root.

Taurus and the Value of the Body

Another important lesson of Taurus is the recognition of the body as a sacred vessel of experience.

The soul does not exist apart from the physical world. It learns and grows through sensory experiences, touch, taste, sound, sight, and smell.

Taurus encourages us to appreciate the beauty and richness of life through these senses. It reminds us that spiritual awareness does not require rejecting the physical world but rather embracing it with gratitude.

Food, music, art, nature, and physical comfort all fall within the realm of Taurus. These pleasures are not distractions from the soul's journey; they are part of it.

Through the senses, we learn to appreciate the miracle of existence.

Taurus and the Meaning of Value

As the soul develops in the Taurus stage, it begins to form a sense of value.

What is truly important? What deserves care and protection?

This stage teaches us about possessions, resources, and personal worth. However, the deeper lesson of Taurus is not merely about material wealth but about recognizing the true value of life itself.

Through experience, the soul gradually learns that the most meaningful treasures are not objects but qualities such as love, trust, beauty, and connection.

Taurus helps us understand what is worth holding onto and what is not.

The Shadow of Taurus

Like every sign of the zodiac, Taurus carries both light and shadow.

When its energy becomes unbalanced, the desire for stability may turn into stubbornness or resistance to change. The comfort Taurus seeks may become attachment to material possessions or habits that no longer serve growth.

Fear of loss can lead to clinging too tightly to what is familiar.

Yet the shadow of Taurus also contains an important lesson: true security does not come from holding onto things but from cultivating inner strength and resilience.

When the Taurus energy is balanced, it provides stability without rigidity and abundance without attachment.

The Gift of Taurus

The great gift of Taurus is endurance.

While Aries provides the courage to begin, Taurus provides the patience to continue. It reminds the soul that meaningful growth requires time, effort, and care.

Taurus teaches us to nurture what we create.

Whether it is a relationship, a family, a garden, or a dream, the Taurus spirit understands that lasting beauty arises from devotion and persistence.

Through this stage of the journey, the soul learns that life is not only about movement and adventure but also about cultivation and care.

Reflection

Consider the areas of your life where you have built stability and nourishment.

What gives you a sense of security?

Where do you find comfort and peace?

The Taurus energy within you encourages appreciation for the simple and profound gifts of life: the beauty of nature, the warmth of connection, and the satisfaction of creating something that endures.

These moments remind us that life's richness often appears in quiet and steady forms.

The Journey Continues

The soul, having learned to root itself in stability through the Taurus stage, now becomes curious about the world around it.

Having established a foundation of security, the next step is exploration and learning.

This curiosity leads the soul into the third stage of the zodiac journey.

It now turns toward the lively and inquisitive energy of Gemini, where the mind awakens, and the quest for knowledge begins.

CHAPTER 3:
GEMINI, THE AWAKENING MIND

THE SYMBOL OF GEMINI ♊

The symbol of Gemini resembles two vertical lines connected at the top and bottom, forming a shape that resembles a gateway or a pair of pillars. These twin pillars represent duality, communication, and the exchange of ideas.

Gemini is symbolized by the Twins, reflecting the dual nature of the mind. It represents the dialogue between different perspectives, the exploration of possibilities, and the constant movement of thought.

Unlike the grounded stillness of Taurus, the Gemini symbol suggests openness and movement. It resembles a doorway through which ideas pass, a bridge between one mind and another.

The Gemini glyph reminds us that knowledge grows through interaction, curiosity, and communication.

Ancient Origins of Gemini

The constellation of Gemini has been recognized for thousands of years and was known to ancient Babylonian astronomers as the "Great Twins." These twin stars, Castor and Pollux, appear close together in the night sky and have long inspired stories about brotherhood, companionship, and shared destiny.

In ancient civilizations, the appearance of Gemini in the sky often coincided with seasons of increased travel and trade. Roads became busier, merchants exchanged goods, and communication between communities flourished.

Because of this, Gemini became associated with movement, exchange, and intellectual curiosity.

It was seen as a symbol of interaction between people and cultures, a reminder that knowledge grows when ideas are shared.

Gemini in Mythology

In Greek mythology, Gemini is associated with the twins Castor and Pollux.

According to legend, these brothers shared a powerful bond. Castor was mortal, while Pollux was the son of Zeus and therefore immortal. When Castor died, Pollux was devastated and asked Zeus to allow them to remain together.

Zeus honored this request by placing the twins in the heavens as the constellation Gemini, allowing them to share immortality.

This myth beautifully symbolizes the Gemini energy of connection and companionship. It reminds us that the mind grows not in isolation but through relationships and shared experiences.

Gemini represents the dialogue between self and other, between question and answer, between curiosity and discovery.

The Awakening of the Mind

After the soul has discovered identity in Aries and stability in Taurus, it begins to notice the world around it.

Questions arise.

What is this place?
Who are these people?
How does everything work?

This stage of the soul's journey marks the awakening of the mind.

Gemini is the sign of curiosity. It encourages exploration, learning, and communication. The soul becomes fascinated by the complexity of life and begins to gather information in order to understand it.

This is the stage where the soul learns the power of language, thought, and ideas.

The Element of Air

Gemini is an air sign, and air represents the realm of intellect, communication, and movement.

Just as the wind travels freely across landscapes, Gemini energy moves quickly through thoughts and conversations.

Air connects everything. It carries sound, spreads seeds, and allows ideas to travel from one person to another.

Through Gemini, the soul learns that communication is a powerful force capable of shaping understanding and building relationships.

Ideas have the ability to inspire change.

Curiosity as a Path to Wisdom

The central lesson of Gemini is curiosity.

Children naturally embody this stage of the soul's journey. They ask endless questions, explore their surroundings, and eagerly absorb new information.

Curiosity is not merely a desire for knowledge; it is a fundamental part of human growth.

Without curiosity, learning would cease.

Gemini reminds us that wisdom begins with the willingness to ask questions and remain open to new possibilities.

The mind expands when it explores unfamiliar territory.

Gemini and the Power of Communication

One of the greatest gifts of Gemini is the ability to communicate.

Through language, humans share ideas, stories, and discoveries. Communication allows individuals to collaborate, innovate, and understand one another.

Gemini energy encourages the exchange of thoughts and perspectives.

It teaches the soul that communication is not only about speaking but also about listening.

True understanding arises when dialogue flows in both directions.

The Dual Nature of the Mind

The symbol of the twins reflects an important aspect of the Gemini stage: the recognition that reality often contains multiple perspectives.

Gemini teaches us that truth is rarely simple or singular. Instead, it invites us to explore different viewpoints and consider possibilities that may initially seem contradictory.

The mind learns to hold opposing ideas and examine them thoughtfully.

This duality can sometimes create restlessness or indecision. The Gemini mind is constantly analyzing, questioning, and exploring alternatives.

Yet this dynamic quality is also what makes Gemini such a powerful force for intellectual growth.

The Shadow of Gemini

Every zodiac sign contains both strengths and challenges.

When Gemini energy becomes unbalanced, curiosity may turn into distraction. The mind may become scattered, jumping from one idea to another without completing any of them.

Excessive mental activity can lead to overthinking or superficial understanding.

The Gemini shadow reminds us that knowledge must be integrated, not merely collected.

True wisdom arises when the mind learns to focus and apply what it has learned.

The Gift of Gemini

The great gift of Gemini is understanding through communication.

It teaches the soul how to express ideas, share experiences, and connect with others through language.

Through Gemini, the mind becomes a bridge between individuals, cultures, and generations.

Ideas spread across time and space, allowing humanity to grow collectively.

Gemini reminds us that learning is a lifelong journey and that curiosity is one of the most powerful forces in human evolution.

Reflection

Think about the moments in your life when curiosity led you toward discovery.

What questions shaped your path?

What conversations opened your mind to new possibilities?

The Gemini energy within you encourages exploration and dialogue.

It reminds us that understanding grows through communication and that every question has the potential to reveal a new dimension of truth.

The Journey Continues

The soul has now awakened its identity through Aries, rooted itself in the physical world through Taurus, and opened its mind through Gemini.

Yet knowledge alone does not fulfill the soul.

The next stage of the journey brings the awakening of the heart.

The soul now turns toward the nurturing and emotional wisdom of Cancer, where the lessons of love, belonging, and emotional connection begin to unfold.

CHAPTER 4:
CANCER, THE AWAKENING OF THE HEART

THE SYMBOL OF CANCER ♋

The symbol of Cancer resembles two curved shapes forming a circle, often interpreted as the claws of a crab or the spiral of life unfolding inward and outward. This image reflects the cyclical nature of emotions, the protective instincts of the heart, and the deep connection between inner and outer experience.

Cancer is symbolized by the Crab, a creature that carries its home with it wherever it goes. The crab moves between land and sea, representing the balance between the physical world and the emotional realm.

This symbol reminds us that the heart is both strong and sensitive, capable of protecting what it loves while remaining open to the tides of feeling that move through life.

Ancient Origins of Cancer

The constellation of Cancer has been known since ancient times, appearing in the star charts of Babylonian and Greek astronomers. In the sky, Cancer sits between Gemini and Leo, marking the point in the zodiac cycle where the Sun reaches its greatest height during the summer solstice in the northern hemisphere.

For ancient civilizations, the summer solstice represented the fullness of life. Crops were growing, warmth filled the air, and the earth seemed to overflow with vitality.

Cancer came to symbolize nurturing, protection, and the sustaining power of life, much like the earth itself during the height of summer.

This connection between Cancer and nourishment gave the sign a deeply maternal quality. It became associated with the care and protection that allow life to flourish.

Cancer in Mythology

In Greek mythology, Cancer appears in the story of Hercules and the Hydra.

During Hercules' battle with the many-headed Hydra, the goddess Hera sent a crab to distract and challenge him. Although the crab was ultimately defeated, Hera honored its loyalty and courage by placing it among the stars as the constellation Cancer.

This myth reflects an important aspect of Cancer energy: loyalty and devotion.

Cancer represents the willingness to protect and defend those we love. Its strength lies not in aggression but in the deep emotional bonds that connect individuals to one another.

The Awakening of Emotion

After the soul learns to think and communicate in the Gemini stage, it begins to discover something deeper.

Thought alone cannot satisfy the soul.

The next stage of growth introduces emotion.

Cancer represents the moment when the soul becomes aware of feelings, love, empathy, compassion, and the desire for belonging. The individual begins to understand that life is not only an intellectual experience but also an emotional one.

Through Cancer, the heart awakens.

The Element of Water

Cancer is the first water sign of the zodiac, and water symbolizes emotion, intuition, and sensitivity.

Water flows, adapts, and responds to its environment. In the same way, emotions move through us, shaping our experiences and relationships.

The water element teaches the soul the importance of empathy and emotional awareness.

Through Cancer, the individual learns to feel deeply and to recognize the emotional connections that bind people together.

Home and Belonging

One of the central themes of Cancer is the concept of home.

Home is more than a physical place. It represents safety, familiarity, and the sense of being accepted and understood.

During the Cancer stage of the soul's journey, the individual begins to seek emotional security and meaningful connection with others.

This stage often corresponds to the development of family bonds, friendships, and the desire to care for loved ones.

Cancer teaches us that human beings thrive when they feel supported and nurtured.

Memory and the Past

Cancer is closely connected with memory and the past.

Our earliest experiences shape the way we see the world and influence the emotional patterns we carry throughout life. Cancer energy invites the soul to reflect on these roots and to understand how they have shaped our identity.

Memories hold powerful emotional energy.

Some memories bring comfort and joy, while others may carry pain or longing. Cancer encourages us to honor these memories while learning to grow beyond them.

Through understanding the past, we gain insight into who we are and how we can move forward with greater compassion.

The Protective Heart

Just as the crab carries its shell for protection, Cancer energy often expresses itself through emotional defense.

When the heart is vulnerable, it naturally seeks safety.

Cancer teaches the soul how to protect what is precious: love, family, and emotional well-being. This protective instinct can be one of Cancer's greatest strengths.

However, the challenge is to protect the heart without closing it completely.

True emotional growth requires both security and openness.

The Shadow of Cancer

Every sign of the zodiac carries both light and shadow.

When Cancer energy becomes unbalanced, emotional sensitivity may turn into moodiness or withdrawal. The desire for security may lead to clinging to the past or resisting necessary change.

Fear of emotional pain can cause individuals to build walls around their hearts.

Yet the shadow of Cancer also holds an important lesson: emotional strength comes from understanding and accepting our feelings, not from avoiding them.

By learning to face emotions with courage and compassion, the soul becomes more resilient and wise.

The Gift of Cancer

The greatest gift of Cancer is compassion.

This sign teaches the soul how to nurture life, to care for others, and to create environments where love can grow.

Cancer reminds us that human beings are not meant to live in isolation. We flourish through connection, empathy, and shared experience.

The heart becomes a source of strength rather than vulnerability.

Through the Cancer stage of the journey, the soul discovers the profound power of love and belonging.

Reflection

Consider the people and places that give you a sense of home.

Who are the individuals who have nurtured and supported you throughout your life?

What memories have shaped the way you experience love and connection?

The Cancer energy within you invites you to honor these emotional roots while continuing to grow and expand your capacity for compassion.

The Journey Continues

The soul has now awakened its identity through Aries, established stability through Taurus, explored the world through Gemini, and opened its heart through Cancer.

Yet the journey of growth continues.

Having discovered emotion and belonging, the soul now seeks to express itself with confidence and creativity.

The next stage of the zodiac journey leads to Leo, where the radiant light of the individual spirit begins to shine.

CHAPTER 5:
LEO, THE RADIANCE OF THE SOUL

THE SYMBOL OF LEO ♌

The symbol of Leo resembles the flowing mane of a lion or a spiral emerging from a central point. This elegant form reflects the outward expression of life force, energy radiating from the center of the self.

Leo is symbolized by the Lion, long regarded as the king of animals. Across many ancient cultures, the lion represented courage, nobility, protection, and royal authority.

The Leo symbol reminds us that within every person lives a spark of divine fire, a creative force waiting to be expressed.

Where Cancer represents the nurturing heart, Leo represents the radiant spirit.

The Ancient Origins of Leo

Leo has been recognized as a powerful constellation since ancient times. The Babylonians, Egyptians, and Greeks all recorded the lion-shaped star pattern in their celestial maps.

The constellation rises prominently during the heat of summer, when the Sun's power is strongest. Because of this connection, Leo became permanently associated with the Sun, the central star that sustains life on Earth.

In astrology, the Sun represents:

- Identity
- Vitality
- Creative power
- Purpose

- The core of the self

Leo therefore reflects the moment in the zodiac journey when the soul becomes aware of its own creative authority and individuality.

Just as the Sun radiates light outward to nourish the world, Leo encourages the individual to radiate their gifts into life.

Leo in Mythology

One of the most famous myths associated with Leo is the story of the Nemean Lion, a legendary creature in Greek mythology.

The Nemean Lion was said to possess an impenetrable golden hide that could not be pierced by weapons. It terrorized the countryside until the hero Hercules confronted it as the first of his twelve labors.

Unable to harm the lion with arrows or swords, Hercules used his strength and courage to defeat the creature in direct combat.

Afterward, Hercules wore the lion's skin as armor, symbolizing the power gained through courage and personal mastery.

The myth carries a deeper meaning: the lion represents the raw power of life itself, and the hero represents the human soul learning to master and channel that power.

In the Leo stage of development, the soul must learn to harness its strength without being consumed by ego or pride.

The Element of Fire

Leo is a fire sign, and fire symbolizes inspiration, passion, and the creative spark that drives life forward.

Fire warms, illuminates, and transforms. Without fire, life would lack energy and momentum.

In the Leo phase of the soul's journey, individuals feel a growing desire to express themselves boldly. Creativity becomes essential, not as a luxury, but as a natural expression of the soul's vitality.

Fire energy encourages us to:

- Create
- Inspire
- Lead
- Celebrate life

Leo reminds us that the soul was not meant to hide in darkness. It was meant to shine.

The Awakening of Creative Power

In Aries the soul discovered existence.
In Taurus it learned stability.
In Gemini it learned to think and communicate.
In Cancer it learned to feel.
Now, in Leo, the soul begins to ask a powerful question:
Who am I meant to become?

Leo represents the stage where individuals start exploring their talents, passions, and creative expression.

This may appear through many forms:

- Art
- Performance
- Leadership
- Writing
- Teaching
- Innovation
- Personal style and identity

Creativity becomes a pathway through which the soul communicates its unique presence to the world.

The Courage to Be Seen

One of Leo's greatest lessons is visibility.

To express oneself fully requires courage.

Many people hesitate to reveal their true gifts out of fear, fear of criticism, rejection, or failure.

Leo teaches the soul that hiding one's light prevents the world from receiving its gifts.

The lion does not ask permission to roar.

It simply exists with confidence.

Through Leo energy, individuals learn to step forward, claim their place in life, and allow their natural talents to emerge.

Leadership and Responsibility

Leo is often associated with leadership.

But true leadership is not about domination or control. Instead, it involves inspiring others through example, warmth, and integrity.

The Sun does not compete with the stars, it simply shines.

In the same way, Leo leadership arises naturally when a person expresses their authentic self.

People are drawn to individuals who embody confidence, generosity, and enthusiasm.

The highest expression of Leo leadership is encouraging others to shine as well.

The Joy of Life

Leo also represents the joy of living.

While some zodiac signs focus on responsibility or survival, Leo reminds us that life is meant to be celebrated.

This energy brings:

- Playfulness
- Laughter
- Celebration
- Creativity
- Romance
- Personal pride

The soul, after exploring emotions through Cancer, now rediscovers the joy of existence.

Children often embody Leo energy naturally. They laugh freely, imagine boldly, and express themselves without hesitation.

Leo invites adults to reconnect with that same playful spirit.

The Shadow of Leo

Like all zodiac signs, Leo has both light and shadow.

When the Leo energy becomes unbalanced, the desire for recognition may turn into arrogance, attention-seeking, or excessive pride.

The ego may become inflated, causing individuals to seek admiration rather than authentic expression.

At its worst, the shadow of Leo can lead to:

- Vanity
- Domination
- Drama
- Self-centeredness

However, these tendencies arise only when the individual forgets that their creative gifts are meant to serve life, not dominate it.

True Leo energy shines brightest when it uplifts others.

The Gift of Leo

At its highest level, Leo represents the radiant heart of the soul.

It is the stage where individuals discover their personal brilliance and begin sharing it with the world.

The gift of Leo is the realization that every human being carries a unique light within them.

When that light is expressed through creativity, courage, and generosity, life becomes richer not only for the individual but for everyone around them.

Leo teaches us that the purpose of life is not merely to exist, but to live vibrantly and wholeheartedly.

Reflection

Where in your life do you feel the desire to express yourself more boldly?

What talents or passions have you felt called to explore but may have held back?

Leo energy invites you to step forward with confidence and allow your creativity to emerge.

The world benefits when individuals share their unique gifts.

Your light has meaning.

The Journey Continues

The soul has now discovered its identity, stability, curiosity, emotional depth, and creative expression.

But growth does not stop with self-expression.

The next stage of the zodiac journey introduces something equally important: refinement and mastery.

After learning to shine, the soul must learn to improve and perfect its gifts.

This leads us into the next sign of the zodiac:

Virgo, the path of wisdom through refinement and service

CHAPTER 6:
VIRGO, THE PATH OF WISDOM THROUGH REFINEMENT

THE SYMBOL OF VIRGO ♍

The symbol of Virgo resembles the letter "M" with a curl or loop at the end. This form has been interpreted in several ways throughout history. Some see it as representing a sheaf of wheat, symbolizing harvest and nourishment. Others see it as representing the unfolding of knowledge, where wisdom grows inward before being shared outward.

Virgo is symbolized by the Maiden, a figure representing purity, intelligence, and devotion to meaningful work. Unlike many mythological maidens who symbolize innocence, Virgo's maiden represents clarity of mind and integrity of purpose.

The symbol reflects Virgo's true essence: discernment, wisdom, and careful attention to life's details.

Ancient Origins of Virgo

Virgo is one of the oldest recognized constellations in human history. It has appeared in the star maps of Babylonian, Greek, and Egyptian civilizations for thousands of years.

In the night sky, Virgo is associated with the bright star Spica, whose name means "ear of wheat." This connection to wheat and harvest made Virgo strongly associated with agriculture and the cycles of nourishment that sustain life.

Ancient societies saw Virgo as a symbol of the earth's abundance and the careful stewardship required to sustain it.

Just as farmers must cultivate, tend, and harvest crops with patience and skill, Virgo represents the human capacity to cultivate knowledge, skill, and wisdom.

Virgo in Mythology

In Greek mythology, Virgo is often linked to Demeter, the goddess of the harvest, and her daughter Persephone.

Demeter represented the nurturing power of the earth and the careful cultivation required to bring life from the soil. Persephone's journey between the underworld and the surface world symbolized the cycles of growth, death, and renewal that govern nature.

Virgo embodies this cycle of careful cultivation.

It reminds us that growth rarely happens through sudden bursts of energy alone. Instead, true development often requires patience, attention, and dedication.

Virgo teaches the soul how to nurture growth in practical and meaningful ways.

The Element of Earth

Virgo is an earth sign, representing stability, practicality, and connection with the physical world.

Earth energy brings structure and grounding to the creative fire of Leo. While Leo inspires bold expression, Virgo asks a deeper question:

How can this creative power be used in a meaningful way?

Virgo helps transform inspiration into real results.

It represents:

- Skill
- Craftsmanship

- Healing
- Organization
- Refinement
- thoughtful service

Where fire ignites passion, earth shapes it into something useful and last.

The Awakening of Purpose

In the Virgo stage of the soul's journey, individuals begin to examine their talents and abilities more carefully.

Instead of simply expressing creativity, the soul now asks:

How can my gifts improve the world around me?

Virgo represents the beginning of purposeful work.

This stage often involves:

- learning practical skills
- developing discipline
- improving health and habits
- seeking meaningful service

The soul begins to understand that fulfillment comes not only from expression but also from contribution.

The Power of Attention

One of Virgo's greatest strengths is attention to detail.

While other signs focus on broad vision or emotional connection, Virgo excels at observing the small elements that others overlook.

This careful observation allows Virgo energy to detect:

- patterns

- inefficiencies
- imbalances
- opportunities for improvement

This is why Virgo energy is often connected to professions involving healing, teaching, research, analysis, and craftsmanship.

Virgo understands that even small adjustments can lead to powerful transformation.

Virgo and Healing

Virgo has long been associated with healing and health.

In astrology, Virgo governs the digestive system, the part of the body responsible for processing and assimilating nourishment. Symbolically, Virgo also represents the mind's ability to digest information and transform it into wisdom.

This connection explains why Virgo energy is drawn toward healing practices.

Virgo seeks to understand how systems function and how they can be improved.

This includes:

- physical health
- emotional well-being
- environmental balance
- spiritual development

The Virgo path encourages the soul to become a steward of well-being.

The Gift of Service

Service is one of Virgo's most profound teachings.

But true service is not about sacrifice or self-neglect. Instead, it arises from recognizing the interconnectedness of life.

When individuals refine their talents and apply them thoughtfully, they naturally contribute to the greater good.

Virgo energy reminds us that meaningful service can appear in many forms:

- teaching others
- creating systems that improve life
- healing the body or mind
- caring for the environment
- sharing knowledge

Through service, the soul discovers that fulfillment often comes from helping life flourish around us.

The Shadow of Virgo

Like every zodiac sign, Virgo also carries challenges.

Because Virgo sees details so clearly, it can sometimes become overly critical, both of others and of itself.

This may lead to:

- perfectionism
- excessive worry
- self-doubt
- overthinking

The Virgo mind may constantly seek improvement, making it difficult to feel satisfied with progress.

However, this shadow contains an important lesson.

Virgo must learn that perfection is not the goal. Growth is.

When Virgo energy embraces compassion and patience, its ability to improve systems and support healing becomes extraordinary.

The Gift of Virgo

At its highest level, Virgo represents the sacred act of refinement.

It teaches the soul how to take raw inspiration and shape it into something meaningful, beneficial, and enduring.

Virgo reminds us that wisdom grows through careful attention, dedication, and a genuine desire to improve life.

The Virgo path transforms creativity into purposeful mastery.

Through this process, the soul learns humility, patience, and devotion to meaningful work.

Reflection

Consider the talents and abilities you have developed throughout your life.

How might these gifts be refined or improved?

In what ways could your knowledge or skills help others grow, heal, or thrive?

Virgo energy invites you to see your abilities not only as personal achievements but also as tools for meaningful contribution.

The Journey Continues

The soul has now moved through identity, stability, curiosity, emotional awareness, creative expression, and refinement.

Yet life continues to expand.

The next stage of the zodiac journey introduces a powerful new lesson:

balance and relationship.

After learning to cultivate personal purpose, the soul must now learn how to share life with others in harmony.

This leads us to the next sign of the zodiac:

Libra, the path of balance, beauty, and partnership.

CHAPTER 7: LIBRA, THE PATH OF BALANCE & SACRED RELATIONSHIP

THE SYMBOL OF LIBRA ♎

The symbol of Libra resembles a horizon line with the rising arc of the Sun above it. It also resembles a balanced scale, representing fairness, equilibrium, and justice.

Libra is the only zodiac sign symbolized not by an animal or mythological figure but by an object, the scales of balance.

This symbol reflects Libra's central lesson: the search for harmony between opposing forces.

Just as scales measure equal weight, Libra seeks balance between:

- self and others
- giving and receiving
- logic and emotion
- independence and connection

Libra reminds the soul that life becomes most beautiful when opposing forces are brought into peaceful harmony.

The Ancient Origins of Libra

Libra's constellation has been recognized since ancient Babylonian times. Early astronomers associated the stars of Libra with the scales of justice, reflecting humanity's enduring desire for fairness and order.

In Roman mythology, Libra became associated with Justitia, the goddess of justice, who holds scales to weigh truth and fairness.

The placement of Libra in the zodiac also carries symbolic meaning. Libra marks the time of the autumn equinox, when day and night become equal in length.

This moment of perfect balance between light and darkness reflects the deeper lesson of Libra: equilibrium between opposing energies.

Libra in Mythology

Many ancient traditions connect Libra with the idea of divine justice and harmony.

In Egyptian mythology, the goddess Ma'at presided over truth, balance, and cosmic order. In the afterlife, a person's heart was weighed against the feather of Ma'at to determine whether they had lived a life of integrity.

This symbolic weighing of the heart represents the universal human desire to live in alignment with truth and fairness.

Libra embodies this principle of ethical balance, encouraging individuals to seek harmony not only in relationships but also within themselves.

The Element of Air

Libra is an air sign, associated with intellect, communication, and perception.

While Gemini represents curiosity and information, Libra represents understanding and perspective.

Air energy allows Libra to step back and view situations from multiple angles. This ability to consider different viewpoints helps Libra seek compromise and cooperation.

Libra teaches the soul that harmony often arises when individuals are willing to listen, reflect, and understand one another.

The Awakening of Relationship

After developing the self through the first six signs of the zodiac, the soul now enters a stage of growth centered on relationships.

Libra represents the moment when the individual recognizes that life is enriched through connection with others.

Relationships become mirrors that reveal deeper aspects of ourselves.

Through relationships, we learn:

- empathy
- compromise
- cooperation
- emotional intelligence

Libra reminds us that relationships are not merely social arrangements; they are pathways for personal evolution.

The Art of Balance

Balance is one of Libra's most important teachings.

Life constantly presents opposing forces:

- independence and unity
- strength and vulnerability
- ambition and rest
- logic and emotion

Libra seeks to integrate these forces rather than allowing one to dominate the other.

This balance does not mean perfection or rigidity. Instead, it is a dynamic process of adjustment, similar to the way scales gently shift until equilibrium is reached.

Through Libra energy, the soul learns that balance is not static; it is a living process of awareness and adjustment.

Beauty and Harmony

Libra is ruled by Venus, the planet associated with beauty, love, and artistic expression.

Because of this influence, Libra has a deep appreciation for aesthetics and harmony.

Libra energy is often drawn toward:

- art
- music
- architecture
- fashion
- design
- elegant environments

This attraction to beauty is not superficial. It reflects a deeper desire to bring order and harmony into the world.

Beauty, for Libra, is a reflection of balance made visible.

The Power of Cooperation

While some signs emphasize independence or ambition, Libra teaches the power of collaboration.

Through cooperation, individuals can achieve outcomes that would be impossible alone.

This cooperative spirit encourages diplomacy and peaceful resolution of conflict.

Libra reminds us that many problems in the world arise not from differences themselves but from the inability to respect those differences.

True harmony requires understanding that diversity can enrich life rather than threaten it.

The Shadow of Libra

Every zodiac sign contains both light and shadow.

When Libra energy becomes unbalanced, the desire for harmony may turn into avoidance of conflict.

In trying to maintain peace, Libra may sometimes suppress its own needs or opinions.

This can lead to:

- indecision
- people-pleasing
- dependence on external approval

Libra must learn that true balance includes honoring one's own truth while respecting the perspectives of others.

Authentic harmony requires honesty and self-respect, not merely agreement.

The Gift of Libra

At its highest expression, Libra represents the beauty of balanced connection.

It teaches the soul how to create relationships that are based on mutual respect, understanding, and shared growth.

Libra reminds us that the most fulfilling partnerships arise when individuals support each other's evolution.

The gift of Libra is the realization that harmony is not something imposed from outside, it emerges naturally when individuals live with fairness, compassion, and integrity.

Reflection

Consider the relationships in your life.

Which relationships bring balance, understanding, and growth?

Are there areas where greater honesty or communication could deepen harmony?

Libra energy encourages reflection on the ways we relate to others and invites us to cultivate relationships rooted in mutual respect and shared purpose.

The Journey Continues

The soul has now explored identity, stability, learning, emotional depth, creativity, refinement, and relationship.

But the journey continues into deeper territory.

After learning the art of balance, the soul must confront something more mysterious and transformative.

The next stage introduces the power of depth, transformation, and hidden truth.

This leads us to the next sign of the zodiac:

Scorpio, the path of transformation and the awakening of inner power.

CHAPTER 8: SCORPIO, THE ALCHEMY OF TRANSFORMATION

THE SYMBOL OF SCORPIO ♏

The symbol of Scorpio resembles the letter “M” ending in a rising arrow or tail. This upward-pointing motion symbolizes energy that begins deep within and rises toward transformation.

Scorpio is traditionally represented by the Scorpion, a creature known for its protective armor and powerful sting. Yet the symbolism of Scorpio goes far beyond this single animal.

Throughout history, Scorpio has also been associated with three stages of transformation:

The Scorpion – representing survival and instinct
The Eagle – representing elevated perception and power
The Phoenix – representing rebirth through transformation

These three symbols describe the evolution of Scorpio energy as the soul learns to move beyond fear and into spiritual renewal.

Ancient Origins of Scorpio

Scorpio has been one of the most recognizable constellations since the earliest star maps of ancient civilizations.

The Babylonians, Egyptians, and Greeks all observed the distinctive pattern of stars forming the Scorpion in the night sky. Because of its striking appearance, Scorpio quickly became associated with powerful mythological stories involving struggle, death, and rebirth.

In the heavens, Scorpio lies opposite the constellation Taurus, symbolizing the eternal tension between creation and transformation.

While Taurus represents the building of life's foundation, Scorpio represents the necessary process of change that allows life to evolve.

Ancient astrologers understood that transformation is not a disruption of life's order; it is part of the natural rhythm of existence.

Scorpio in Mythology

In Greek mythology, Scorpio appears in the famous story of Orion, the mighty hunter.

According to the legend, Orion boasted that he could defeat any creature on Earth. In response to his arrogance, the goddess Gaia sent a giant scorpion to challenge him.

The scorpion ultimately defeated Orion, and both figures were placed in the sky as constellations. To this day, when Scorpio rises in the night sky, Orion sets below the horizon.

This myth symbolizes a deeper truth: no force of life can remain unchanged forever.

Scorpio represents the humbling realization that transformation is inevitable. Through transformation, the soul gains wisdom and resilience.

The Element of Water

Scorpio is a water sign, but unlike the gentle emotional waters of Cancer or the dreamy currents of Pisces, Scorpio represents deep and powerful emotional currents.

These waters flow beneath the surface, carrying the mysteries of the subconscious mind.

Scorpio energy is associated with:

- emotional intensity
- psychological depth

- intuition
- passion
- spiritual transformation

The waters of Scorpio are not calm lakes, they are deep oceans where hidden truths reside.

To navigate these waters requires courage and self-awareness.

The Awakening of Inner Power

In the Scorpio stage of the soul's journey, individuals begin to confront deeper aspects of themselves.

This includes exploring emotions and experiences that may have been buried or ignored.

Scorpio asks powerful questions:

What fears shape your decisions?
What emotional wounds still influence your life?
What truths have you avoided facing?

While these questions may feel uncomfortable, they are essential for transformation.

Scorpio teaches that true power comes from understanding the hidden forces within ourselves.

Life, Death, and Rebirth

One of Scorpio's most profound teachings is the cycle of death and rebirth.

This concept does not only refer to physical death but to the many symbolic endings and beginnings that occur throughout life.

Every major transformation involves letting go of something old so that something new can emerge.

Examples include:

- leaving old beliefs behind
- ending unhealthy relationships
- releasing emotional pain
- transforming identity and purpose

Scorpio reminds us that endings are not failures; they are gateways to renewal.

The Phoenix, rising from its ashes, perfectly symbolizes this process.

Emotional Depth and Intimacy

Scorpio is strongly associated with emotional intensity and deep connection.

While Libra introduced the importance of relationships, Scorpio explores the depth and authenticity of those connections.

Superficial interactions rarely satisfy Scorpio energy. Instead, Scorpio seeks relationships built on honesty, vulnerability, and trust.

Through deep emotional bonds, individuals experience powerful opportunities for growth and healing.

Scorpio teaches that true intimacy requires the courage to reveal one's authentic self.

The Hidden World

Another dimension of Scorpio involves the exploration of hidden knowledge.

Throughout history, Scorpio has been associated with:

- psychology
- mysticism

- spiritual transformation
- secret knowledge
- life's deeper mysteries

This sign often inspires individuals to explore subjects that lie beyond the surface of ordinary experience.

Many people influenced by Scorpio energy feel drawn to fields such as:

- healing arts
- investigative work
- spiritual study
- research and discovery

Scorpio's curiosity is not satisfied with simple explanations. It seeks to uncover the truth beneath appearances.

The Shadow of Scorpio

Scorpio's depth and intensity can sometimes lead to challenges.

When Scorpio energy becomes unbalanced, emotional intensity may transform into:

- jealousy
- possessiveness
- resentment
- secrecy
- manipulation

Because Scorpio feels emotions so deeply, it may struggle with trust or fear of vulnerability.

Yet these challenges also hold the key to Scorpio's greatest strength.

By learning to release fear and embrace transformation, Scorpio energy becomes one of the most powerful forces for personal growth.

The Gift of Scorpio

At its highest expression, Scorpio represents the alchemist of the zodiac.

Alchemy is the ancient practice of transforming base elements into gold. Symbolically, Scorpio performs this transformation within the human soul.

Through courage and self-awareness, Scorpio teaches us to transform:

- pain into wisdom
- fear into strength
- endings into new beginnings

The gift of Scorpio is the realization that transformation is not something to fear, it is the very process through which life evolves.

Reflection

Consider moments in your life when you experienced profound change.

What challenges forced you to grow or transform?

What lessons emerged from those experiences?

Scorpio energy invites you to recognize the hidden power within every transformation.

Even the most difficult transitions can lead to greater understanding and renewal.

The Journey Continues

The soul has now explored identity, stability, knowledge, emotion, creativity, refinement, relationship, and transformation.

But the journey continues to expand toward greater wisdom.

After the deep emotional and psychological transformations of Scorpio, the soul begins to seek a broader understanding of life’s meaning.

CHAPTER 9: SAGITTARIUS, THE QUEST FOR TRUTH & EXPANSION

THE SYMBOL OF SAGITTARIUS ␐

The symbol of Sagittarius is an arrow pointed upward, representing direction, purpose, and the pursuit of higher truth. The arrow reminds us that Sagittarius energy is always reaching beyond the present moment toward something greater.

Sagittarius is symbolized by the Archer, traditionally depicted as a centaur, half human and half horse, drawing a bow toward the sky.

The centaur represents the union of instinct and intellect, while the arrow symbolizes the human desire to aim for higher knowledge and spiritual understanding.

Sagittarius teaches that life is a journey of discovery, and every experience can lead us closer to truth.

Ancient Origins of Sagittarius

The constellation of Sagittarius has been recognized by ancient civilizations for thousands of years. Babylonian astronomers identified the star pattern as a powerful archer guarding the gateway to the center of the Milky Way.

Interestingly, the direction of Sagittarius in the night sky points toward the galactic center, the powerful gravitational core of our galaxy.

For ancient observers, this region of the sky symbolized a cosmic doorway, a place where divine knowledge and universal wisdom could be accessed.

This celestial alignment beautifully reflects Sagittarius' role in the zodiac: the seeker of universal truth.

Sagittarius in Mythology

In Greek mythology, Sagittarius is often associated with Chiron, the wise centaur.

Unlike other centaurs known for wild behavior, Chiron was revered for his intelligence, compassion, and deep knowledge. He became a teacher to heroes such as Achilles and Hercules, guiding them in medicine, philosophy, and combat.

Chiron represents the teacher archetype, the individual who gains wisdom through experience and then shares that wisdom with others.

This myth reveals an important dimension of Sagittarius energy: the desire not only to discover truth but also to teach and inspire others.

The Element of Fire

Sagittarius is a fire sign, like Aries and Leo, but its fire expresses itself differently.

Where Aries ignites action and Leo expresses creative radiance, Sagittarius uses fire as the flame of curiosity and exploration.

This fire fuels the desire to:

- travel
- study philosophy
- explore cultures
- seek spiritual understanding
- ask profound questions about existence

Sagittarius energy thrives when life becomes an adventure of learning and discovery.

The Awakening of Wisdom

In the Sagittarius stage of the soul's journey, the individual begins searching for meaning beyond personal experiences.

After confronting transformation in Scorpio, the soul now asks:

Why do these experiences occur?
What lessons do they hold?
What truths govern the universe?

Sagittarius represents the stage where individuals begin exploring:

- philosophy
- religion
- spiritual teachings
- higher education
- global cultures

This exploration expands the mind and broadens the soul's perspective.

The Spirit of Exploration

Sagittarius is the zodiac's great explorer.

This exploration may take many forms:

- physical travel across the world
- intellectual exploration through study
- spiritual exploration through meditation or philosophy

The Sagittarius soul seeks to understand life by experiencing it directly.

Travel, both literal and symbolic, becomes a powerful teacher.

By encountering different cultures, ideas, and perspectives, Sagittarius learns that truth is often larger than any single viewpoint.

Optimism and Vision

One of Sagittarius' greatest gifts is optimism.

Even after life's most difficult transformations, Sagittarius believes that growth and meaning can emerge from every experience.

This optimistic vision helps individuals move forward with courage and hope.

Sagittarius energy encourages us to see challenges not as obstacles but as lessons on the path of wisdom.

This hopeful perspective often inspires others and brings enthusiasm to any environment.

Freedom and Independence

Sagittarius values freedom.

This freedom is not simply rebellion against authority but a deeper need to explore life without unnecessary limitations.

Sagittarius energy resists confinement, whether physical, intellectual, or emotional.

The Archer must be able to aim its arrow freely toward the horizon.

This independence allows Sagittarius individuals to pursue truth without fear of challenging existing beliefs or traditions.

The Teacher Within

As Sagittarius grows in wisdom, it naturally develops the desire to share its insights with others.

Many teachers, philosophers, writers, and spiritual guides embody Sagittarius energy.

The role of the teacher is not to impose beliefs but to encourage others to think, question, and explore.

Sagittarius reminds us that knowledge becomes most powerful when it is shared with generosity and humility.

The Shadow of Sagittarius

Like all zodiac signs, Sagittarius also carries potential challenges.

Because Sagittarius loves freedom and exploration, it may sometimes struggle with:

- restlessness
- impatience
- blunt honesty that may hurt others
- overconfidence in personal beliefs

Sagittarius must learn that wisdom requires both curiosity and humility.

True knowledge grows through continuous learning and openness to new perspectives.

The Gift of Sagittarius

At its highest level, Sagittarius represents the philosopher of the zodiac.

It teaches the soul to search for truth with courage, curiosity, and hope.

Sagittarius reminds us that life is not only about survival or personal success, but it is also about understanding the deeper meaning of existence.

Through exploration and reflection, Sagittarius transforms life's experiences into wisdom.

Reflection

Consider the experiences that have expanded your understanding of life.

What journeys, physical, intellectual, or spiritual, have shaped your perspective?

Sagittarius energy invites you to remain curious and open to discovery.

The search for truth is a lifelong journey.

The Journey Continues

The soul has now traveled through identity, stability, learning, emotion, creativity, refinement, relationship, transformation, and philosophical exploration.

Yet the journey is not complete.

After discovering truth, the soul must learn how to apply that wisdom in the world through responsibility and mastery.

The next stage of the zodiac journey brings structure and discipline to the lessons learned so far.

CHAPTER 10: CAPRICORN, THE PATH OF MASTERY & ENDURING LEGACY

THE SYMBOL OF CAPRICORN ♑

The symbol of Capricorn resembles a stylized "V" with a looping tail that curves inward. This symbol represents the unique creature associated with Capricorn: the Sea-Goat.

The Sea-Goat is a mythical being with the body of a goat and the tail of a fish. This unusual combination symbolizes Capricorn's remarkable ability to navigate both the material world and the deeper emotional or spiritual realms.

The goat portion represents determination, ambition, and the ability to climb great heights. The fish tail represents the depths of intuition and emotional wisdom.

Together, these elements symbolize Capricorn's role as the sign that bridges earthly achievement and deeper purpose.

Ancient Origins of Capricorn

Capricorn is one of the oldest recognized constellations in human history. Ancient Babylonian astronomers referred to it as the "Goat-Fish", associating it with divine guardianship and the protection of civilization.

The constellation rises during the winter season in the northern hemisphere, a time when nature appears quiet and dormant. Yet beneath the surface, life is preparing for renewal.

Because of this seasonal symbolism, Capricorn became associated with endurance, patience, and the long cycles of time.

Capricorn energy understands that meaningful accomplishments rarely appear instantly. They are built slowly, through consistent effort and dedication.

Capricorn in Mythology

In Greek mythology, Capricorn is often linked to the god Pan, a creature with the body of a goat.

When the monster Typhon threatened the gods, Pan jumped into a river to escape. As he transformed to survive, his lower body became the tail of a fish.

The gods later placed Pan among the stars as the constellation Capricorn.

This myth symbolizes Capricorn's ability to adapt and survive even in challenging circumstances. Capricorn energy thrives not through sudden bursts of action but through persistence and resilience.

The Element of Earth

Capricorn is an earth sign, representing practicality, structure, and tangible achievement.

Where Virgo refined skills and Taurus built foundations, Capricorn represents the construction of enduring accomplishments.

Earth energy gives Capricorn its ability to remain focused on long-term goals. While other signs may become distracted or impatient, Capricorn remains committed to steady progress.

Capricorn teaches the soul the importance of:

- discipline
- responsibility
- perseverance
- patience

These qualities allow individuals to transform vision into reality.

The Awakening of Responsibility

In the Capricorn stage of the soul's journey, individuals begin to recognize their role within the larger structure of society.

After exploring personal truth in Sagittarius, the soul now asks:

How can I contribute to the world?
What responsibilities do I carry?
What legacy will I leave behind?

Capricorn encourages individuals to take ownership of their lives and their actions.

This stage often involves building careers, creating stable environments, and contributing to communities.

Responsibility becomes a pathway to personal growth.

The Climb Toward Mastery

The image of the mountain goat climbing steep cliffs perfectly captures Capricorn's essence.

The goat does not rush toward the summit. Instead, it moves carefully, placing each step with precision.

In the same way, Capricorn understands that mastery requires time and consistent effort.

This climb may involve overcoming obstacles such as:

- self-doubt
- setbacks
- external challenges
- long periods of hard work

Yet Capricorn possesses an extraordinary ability to endure these difficulties while remaining focused on the ultimate goal.

Time, Wisdom, and Maturity

Capricorn is ruled by Saturn, the planet associated with time, structure, and life lessons.

Saturn's influence encourages patience and maturity. It reminds us that true success is rarely achieved quickly.

Instead, wisdom grows through experience.

Many Capricorn lessons involve learning through challenges and responsibilities. While these experiences may feel demanding, they ultimately lead to greater strength and self-mastery.

Saturn teaches that the rewards of life often come through discipline and perseverance.

Building a Legacy

One of Capricorn's deepest motivations is the desire to create something that lasts beyond one's lifetime.

This legacy may appear through:

- meaningful work
- leadership
- contributions to society
- guiding future generations

Capricorn energy understands that individual actions can shape the future.

By committing to purposeful work and ethical responsibility, individuals create structures that benefit others long after they are gone.

The Shadow of Capricorn

Like every zodiac sign, Capricorn also has challenges.

When Capricorn energy becomes unbalanced, ambition may turn into:

- excessive work
- emotional distance
- fear of failure
- rigid thinking

In some cases, individuals may become so focused on achievement that they neglect emotional connection or personal fulfillment.

Capricorn must learn that true success involves balance between accomplishment and well-being.

Life's greatest achievements are most meaningful when they are accompanied by compassion and wisdom.

The Gift of Capricorn

At its highest level, Capricorn represents the architect of the zodiac.

It teaches the soul how to build structures that endure, both in the external world and within personal character.

Capricorn reminds us that lasting success arises from integrity, patience, and dedication.

Through this sign, the soul learns that purpose is not simply discovered, it is constructed through commitment and perseverance.

Reflection

Consider the long-term goals you are working toward in your life.

What structures or accomplishments are you building that may endure beyond the present moment?

Capricorn energy invites you to reflect on how your actions today contribute to the future you wish to create.

Every step taken with intention brings you closer to mastery.

The Journey Continues

The soul has now traveled through identity, stability, learning, emotion, creativity, refinement, relationship, transformation, exploration, and mastery.

Yet the zodiac journey continues toward a new stage of evolution.

After establishing structure and responsibility through Capricorn, the soul begins to look toward the future and the collective progress of humanity.

CHAPTER 11:
AQUARIUS, THE AWAKENING OF VISION & COLLECTIVE CONSCIOUSNESS

THE SYMBOL OF AQUARIUS ♒

The symbol of Aquarius appears as two flowing waves. These waves are often mistaken for water, but they actually represent the flow of knowledge and energy moving through the world.

Aquarius is symbolized by the Water Bearer, a figure pouring life-giving water from a vessel. However, the water in this image is not ordinary water, it represents wisdom, innovation, and spiritual insight.

The Water Bearer distributes this knowledge freely to humanity, symbolizing the role of Aquarius as a bringer of enlightenment and progress.

Aquarius teaches that knowledge is meant to be shared for the benefit of all.

Ancient Origins of Aquarius

The constellation of Aquarius has been recognized since the earliest days of astronomy. Ancient civilizations associated this constellation with the life-giving waters that nourished their lands.

In Babylonian star lore, Aquarius represented the god Ea, a divine figure associated with wisdom and the flow of cosmic knowledge.

Because water was essential for sustaining life, the Water Bearer became a powerful symbol of renewal and collective well-being.

In astrology, Aquarius represents the distribution of ideas and innovations that help society evolve.

Aquarius in Mythology

In Greek mythology, Aquarius is sometimes associated with Ganymede, a young figure chosen by the gods to serve as the cupbearer of Mount Olympus.

Ganymede was tasked with pouring divine nectar for the gods, symbolizing the sharing of sacred knowledge.

This myth highlights Aquarius' role as a messenger of higher awareness.

Rather than keeping wisdom hidden, Aquarius distributes it freely so that others may grow and evolve.

The Element of Air

Aquarius is an air sign, representing thought, communication, and intellectual exploration.

While Gemini seeks information and Libra seeks balance, Aquarius represents visionary thinking.

Aquarius energy looks beyond current conditions and imagines what the future could become.

It asks questions such as:

How can society improve?
What systems need to change?
What innovations could transform the world?

Aquarius thrives when exploring new possibilities and challenging outdated assumptions.

The Awakening of the Collective Mind

In the Aquarius stage of the soul's journey, individuals begin to move beyond personal goals and consider the well-being of the larger community.

After building personal mastery in Capricorn, the soul now asks:

- How can my abilities contribute to humanity?
- What changes could improve the world?
- How can knowledge be used to uplift society?

Aquarius represents the awakening of collective consciousness, the understanding that humanity is interconnected.

This stage encourages individuals to participate in movements that promote progress, equality, and shared knowledge.

Innovation and Vision

Aquarius is often associated with innovation and breakthrough thinking.

Throughout history, many scientists, inventors, and reformers have embodied Aquarius energy.

This sign inspires the exploration of new ideas in fields such as:

- science
- technology
- social reform

- humanitarian work
- philosophy

Aquarius reminds us that progress occurs when individuals are willing to question established systems and imagine new possibilities.

Freedom and Individuality

One of Aquarius' greatest values is individual freedom.

Aquarius encourages people to express their unique ideas and perspectives without fear of conformity.

While Capricorn builds structures, Aquarius examines those structures and asks whether they still serve humanity's highest good.

If a system becomes outdated or restrictive, Aquarius seeks to transform it.

This spirit of independence helps society evolve and adapt to new realities.

The Power of Community

Although Aquarius values individuality, it also recognizes the importance of community.

True progress often occurs when individuals work together toward shared goals.

Aquarius energy encourages collaboration among diverse groups of people who bring different talents and perspectives.

Through cooperation and open dialogue, communities can develop innovative solutions to complex challenges.

The Shadow of Aquarius

Like all zodiac signs, Aquarius carries potential challenges.

Because Aquarius focuses strongly on ideas and vision, it may sometimes become emotionally detached or overly intellectual.

This can lead to:

- stubborn beliefs
- rebellion without direction
- difficulty relating to emotional needs

Aquarius must remember that progress involves not only ideas but also compassion and understanding.

True innovation should improve life for both individuals and communities.

The Gift of Aquarius

At its highest expression, Aquarius represents the visionary of the zodiac.

It inspires humanity to imagine a future where knowledge, equality, and cooperation guide our actions.

Aquarius reminds us that progress often begins with individuals who dare to think differently.

By sharing ideas and encouraging open exploration, Aquarius energy helps humanity move toward greater awareness and unity.

Reflection

Consider the ways in which your ideas or talents might contribute to the greater good.

Are there causes, innovations, or movements that inspire you to think about the future of humanity?

Aquarius energy invites you to explore how your unique perspective can help shape a more enlightened world.

The Journey Continues

The soul has now traveled through identity, stability, curiosity, emotion, creativity, refinement, relationship, transformation, exploration, mastery, and vision.

Only one stage of the zodiac journey remains.

The final sign represents the merging of all experiences into spiritual understanding and compassion.

CHAPTER 12: PISCES, THE RETURN TO UNITY & THE WISDOM OF THE SOUL

THE SYMBOL OF PISCES ♓

The symbol of Pisces shows two fish swimming in opposite directions, connected by a flowing line. This image represents the dual nature of existence: the pull between the physical world and the spiritual realm.

One fish swims toward the material experience of life, while the other swims toward the infinite ocean of spirit.

The connecting line reminds us that these two forces are not separate. They are part of the same eternal cycle.

Pisces symbolizes the realization that life is both earthly and divine, and the soul moves continuously between these dimensions.

Ancient Origins of Pisces

The constellation of Pisces has been known since the earliest astronomical records of Babylonian and Greek civilizations.

Ancient cultures associated Pisces with the great cosmic ocean, the endless waters from which life emerges and to which it eventually returns.

Because water symbolizes the subconscious and the spiritual world, Pisces became associated with mystery, intuition, and divine connection.

Pisces represents the moment when the soul becomes aware of its place within the greater universe.

Pisces in Mythology

In Greek mythology, Pisces is connected to the story of Aphrodite and Eros, the goddess of love and her son.

When the monstrous Typhon threatened the gods, Aphrodite and Eros transformed themselves into fish and dove into the river to escape. They tied themselves together with a cord so they would not lose each other in the currents.

The gods later honored their unity by placing the fish among the stars as the constellation Pisces.

This myth symbolizes connection, compassion, and protection through unity.

Pisces teaches that even in moments of chaos, love and connection guide the soul safely through life's currents.

The Element of Water

Pisces is a water sign, representing emotion, intuition, and spiritual depth.

While Cancer represents nurturing emotion and Scorpio represents transformative emotion, Pisces represents universal compassion.

Pisces energy dissolves the boundaries between individuals, reminding us that all living beings share the same cosmic origin.

This sign is strongly associated with empathy, creativity, imagination, and spiritual awareness.

Pisces invites the soul to feel the interconnectedness of life.

The Awakening of Compassion

By the time the soul reaches the Pisces stage of the zodiac journey, it has experienced every dimension of human existence.

It has learned identity, stability, knowledge, emotion, creativity, discipline, relationship, transformation, wisdom, responsibility, and collective vision.

With all of these experiences gathered, the soul begins to understand something profound:

Every person is on their own journey of growth.

This realization awakens compassion.

Pisces encourages us to approach others not with judgment, but with understanding and empathy.

The World of Imagination and Spirit

Pisces has long been associated with artistic inspiration and mystical insight.

Many artists, poets, musicians, and spiritual teachers embody Pisces energy.

This sign connects individuals with the deeper currents of imagination and creativity.

Pisces reminds us that creativity is not simply entertainment; it is a channel through which the soul expresses its deepest truths.

Through art, music, writing, and spiritual practice, Pisces allows the invisible dimensions of life to become visible.

The Dissolution of Boundaries

One of Pisces' most unique qualities is its ability to dissolve boundaries.

While other signs emphasize individuality or structure, Pisces invites the soul to transcend these limitations.

This does not mean losing identity but rather understanding that identity exists within a larger universal context.

Pisces encourages the realization that:

- humanity is interconnected
- life is part of a greater cosmic order
- compassion strengthens the world

Through this awareness, individuals may develop a deep desire to contribute to healing and unity.

The Shadow of Pisces

Like every zodiac sign, Pisces also has challenges.

Because Pisces feels emotions and energies so deeply, individuals influenced by this sign may sometimes struggle with:

- escapism
- confusion
- emotional overwhelm
- difficulty maintaining boundaries

When life becomes overwhelming, Pisces energy may attempt to escape reality rather than confront it.

Yet these challenges also carry important lessons.

Pisces must learn that spiritual awareness does not require escaping life; it requires engaging with life compassionately and courageously.

The Gift of Pisces

At its highest expression, Pisces represents the mystic of the zodiac.

It embodies wisdom, compassion, and spiritual awareness.

Pisces teaches that the ultimate purpose of life is not merely success or knowledge, but love and understanding.

Through compassion, the soul recognizes the sacred value of every living being.

This awareness allows individuals to become sources of healing and inspiration for others.

The Completion of the Zodiac Journey

Pisces represents the final stage of the zodiac cycle, but it is also a gateway to renewal.

After the soul integrates the wisdom of Pisces, the cycle begins again with Aries, the rebirth of identity and new experiences.

This continuous cycle reflects the ongoing evolution of life and consciousness.

Each journey through the zodiac deepens the soul's understanding of existence.

Reflection

Consider the experiences that have shaped your life.

What lessons have taught you compassion, understanding, and wisdom?

Pisces invites you to see your life as part of a much larger story, one that connects all living beings through shared experience.

Through compassion and awareness, the soul continues to evolve.

The Journey Continues

As the cycle comes full circle, the Leo lesson remains like a steady flame at the center of the soul's evolution: you were born to shine, not for applause, but to warm the world with what is true in you.

Throughout this journey, you have met every sign as a teacher, yet Leo reminds you that no wisdom is fully lived until it is expressed. Insight becomes embodied when it is carried with dignity, when the heart stays open, and when creative courage is used in the service of love.

When life returns you to beginnings, new seasons, new relationships, new callings, you may notice the same themes appearing again. This is not repetition, but refinement. Each turn of the spiral asks you to let the ego soften while the inner Sun grows brighter: a self that no longer needs to prove its worth, because it knows its worth.

So the journey continues, through your choices, your healing, your relationships, and your creations. And wherever you go next, carry

Leo's highest gift with you: generosity of spirit. Let your light make room for others to shine, and you will discover that the soul's path is not a destination, but an ever-deepening return to the heart.

The Eternal Cycle

The zodiac is more than a system of astrology. It is a symbolic map of human evolution.

From Aries' spark of identity to Pisces' universal compassion, the zodiac reflects the many stages through which the soul grows and learns.

Each sign contributes an essential lesson.

Together, they form a complete journey of transformation.

And just as the seasons return each year, the cycle of the zodiac reminds us that growth is never truly finished.

Every ending carries the seed of a new beginning.

PART II:

THE HOUSES,

THE JOURNEY OF THE SOUL THROUGH LIFE

CHAPTER 13:
THE SPIRAL OF THE SOUL

Astrology is often introduced as a system of signs and symbols that describe personality traits. Yet beneath this surface lies something far more profound.

The zodiac is not simply a set of character descriptions. It is a map of human experience, revealing how the soul grows through the many stages of life.

In the previous section of this book, we explored the twelve zodiac signs as stages of soul evolution. From Aries' awakening of identity to Pisces' return to spiritual unity, the signs describe the development of consciousness.

But knowing who the soul is becoming is only part of the story.

We must also understand where those lessons unfold.

This is where the twelve houses enter the picture.

If the zodiac signs describe the qualities of the traveler, the houses describe the landscape of the journey.

Each house represents a different dimension of life experience: identity, relationships, work, creativity, family, purpose, and spiritual connection.

Together, they create a complete picture of the soul's journey through earthly life.

Life as a Spiral, Not a Circle

Many people imagine the zodiac as a simple circle. Aries begins the cycle, Pisces ends it, and the process repeats endlessly.

But the journey of the soul is not truly circular.

It is spiral-shaped.

Each time we encounter similar experiences in life, we do so with greater understanding. The lessons may appear familiar, yet we are not the same person we were before.

A child learning independence experiences Aries energy differently than an adult beginning a new career or a spiritual seeker starting a new phase of personal growth.

The outer circumstances may resemble previous stages, but the level of awareness has changed.

The spiral represents the continual expansion of consciousness.

Every experience carries the possibility of deeper understanding.

The Twelve Houses as Stages of Life Experience

The houses represent the major areas of life where the soul learns and evolves.

Each house corresponds to a fundamental dimension of human experience.

The First House represents identity and self-expression.

The Second House governs resources, security, and self-worth.

The Third House explores communication, learning, and curiosity.

The Fourth House reflects home, family, and emotional foundations.

The Fifth House celebrates creativity, joy, and the expression of individuality.

The Sixth House focuses on work, health, and service.

The Seventh House explores partnerships and relationships.

The Eighth House introduces transformation, shared resources, and deep emotional change.

The Ninth House expands consciousness through philosophy, travel, and spiritual exploration.

The Tenth House represents career, purpose, and contribution to society.

The Eleventh House reflects community, collective vision, and the future of humanity.

Finally, the Twelfth House represents spiritual integration, compassion, and the connection to the infinite.

Together, these twelve houses describe the full landscape of human life.

The Houses as Windows of Experience

Each person's birth chart arranges the zodiac signs across these twelve houses in a unique pattern.

This pattern reveals how the soul intends to explore life in this particular incarnation.

For one person, creativity may appear as a central theme. For another, relationships or spiritual exploration may take a more prominent role.

The houses help us understand where our greatest lessons, opportunities, and growth experiences are likely to occur.

Rather than predicting rigid outcomes, astrology reveals patterns of potential.

It shows where life may invite us to develop strength, wisdom, and awareness.

The Dance Between Signs and Houses

To truly understand astrology, it is important to see how the signs and houses work together.

The signs describe the energy of the experience.

The houses describe the area of life where that energy appears.

For example:

If Leo represents creativity and self-expression, the Fifth House reveals where that creativity unfolds.

If Scorpio represents transformation, the Eighth House shows where deep emotional change may occur.

This dynamic relationship between signs and houses creates the rich complexity of every individual birth chart.

Each chart becomes a unique map of the soul's journey.

Astrology as a Tool for Self-Awareness

When approached thoughtfully, astrology becomes a powerful tool for self-discovery.

Rather than limiting individuals with fixed labels, it encourages reflection and personal growth.

Through the houses, we begin to ask deeper questions:

Where am I being asked to grow?

Which areas of life challenge me most?

What experiences are shaping my understanding of the world?

These questions help transform astrology from simple curiosity into a guide for conscious living.

The Journey Through the Houses

Just as the zodiac signs follow a natural sequence, the houses also unfold in a meaningful order.

The journey begins with the First House, where the soul discovers identity and personal presence.

It then moves through the development of resources, communication, family, creativity, service, and relationships.

Later houses explore deeper transformation, spiritual understanding, and collective contribution.

Finally, the Twelfth House brings the journey back to the infinite, completing the cycle of life experience.

Each house represents a doorway through which the soul encounters new lessons.

The Invitation to Awareness

Life often presents experiences that seem random or unpredictable. Yet astrology suggests that beneath these events lies a deeper pattern of growth.

The houses remind us that every challenge, opportunity, and relationship can become part of the soul's learning process.

When we become aware of these patterns, we begin to approach life with greater understanding.

We recognize that the experiences we encounter are not merely obstacles or coincidences.

They are invitations to evolve.

The Journey Begins Again

With this understanding, we are ready to explore the houses one by one.

Each chapter that follows will illuminate a different aspect of life's journey.

Together they form a complete map of the soul's experiences in the world.

The journey begins where every life begins, with the discovery of the self.

CHAPTER 14:
THE FIRST HOUSE, AWAKENING THE SELF

Before the soul can understand what it owns, earns, or values, it must first come into contact with something far more profound—it must recognize that it exists. The First House represents this sacred beginning, the moment awareness steps forward into form and declares, "I am." This is not a learned identity or a constructed version of self. It is the raw, unfiltered emergence of being, the first breath of individuality as the soul enters the physical world and takes on a body, a presence, and a unique path.

In this house, the soul is not yet concerned with stability or survival in a material sense. It is not asking what it has or what it is worth. Instead, it is discovering what it feels like to exist as a separate, conscious being. There is a profound innocence here, a kind of spiritual infancy where the focus is on presence, instinct, and immediate experience. The First House asks the most essential question any soul will ever encounter: Who am I? Not in terms of roles or labels, but in essence. Who am I when I stand alone, before expectation, before conditioning, before the world tells me who I should be?

The First House is traditionally associated with Aries, the first sign of the zodiac, and this connection is deeply meaningful. Aries is the spark of life itself—the initiator, the force that begins without hesitation or overthinking. It is bold, instinctive, and driven by an inner impulse that says move forward. Aries does not wait to be understood or approved. It acts because something within it knows that beginning is necessary. This energy mirrors the moment of birth, when life emerges into the world without certainty, without guarantees, but with undeniable presence.

This connection teaches that identity is not something we passively discover. It is something we actively step into. The First House does not promise clarity from the start. Instead, it offers movement, experience, and the courage to explore oneself through action. Just as Aries charges forward, the soul in the First House learns by doing, by trying, by expressing, and sometimes by stumbling. There is no perfection here—only authenticity in motion.

On a practical level, the First House governs the physical body and the way we naturally present ourselves to the world. It influences our appearance, our posture, our gestures, and the immediate impression we make when others encounter us. It is the energy people feel before words are spoken, the silent introduction that says, "This is who I am." Yet beneath this outer layer lies something much deeper. The First House reflects how we experience ourselves from the inside. It shapes our instincts, our reactions, and the way we respond to life in real time.

This is the self before it has been overly shaped by external influence. It is the raw self—the part of us that reacts without overanalyzing, that moves before doubt has time to interfere. It is where intuition lives in its purest form. In many ways, the First House holds the truth of who we are beneath all learned behavior.

As the soul awakens in this house, it begins to understand individuality. There is a shift that takes place, a movement away from collective identity and into personal awareness. The soul starts to recognize itself as distinct, separate, and uniquely expressed. This can feel empowering, but it can also feel vulnerable. To be an individual means to stand on your own, to make choices, to take action, and to face the results of those actions. It is the beginning of personal responsibility, but also the beginning of true freedom.

The First House teaches that you are not here to blend into the background or become a reflection of others. You are here to express something that has never existed before in quite the same way. Your presence is not accidental. It is intentional, even if you do not yet fully understand why.

The body plays a significant role in this house, serving as the vessel through which the soul experiences life. It is through the body that we act, create, communicate, and connect. The First House reminds us that the body is not separate from the self—it is an extension of it. Learning to listen to the body's signals, instincts, and needs becomes an important part of this stage of development. The body often responds before the mind has time to interpret. It knows when something feels safe or unsafe, aligned or misaligned.

To honor the First House is to begin forming a respectful relationship with the body, seeing it not as something to control or criticize, but as a partner in the journey of being alive. It is the home the soul inhabits, and how we treat it reflects how we relate to ourselves.

Another key aspect of the First House is the instinct to begin. This is the house of action, of initiation, of taking that first step even when the outcome is uncertain. It governs the courage required to start something new, whether that is a project, a relationship, a personal transformation, or simply a new way of thinking. The First House does not wait for perfect timing or complete understanding. It moves because movement itself is necessary for growth.

This can be both exhilarating and uncomfortable. Beginning often means stepping into the unknown, leaving behind the safety of what is familiar. Yet without this willingness, nothing new can take shape. The First House teaches that life responds to action. Even small steps create momentum, and momentum creates change.

Like every house, the First House also carries a shadow. When its energy is not fully integrated, it can manifest as fear of being seen or confusion about identity. This may appear as hiding one's true self to avoid judgment, constantly seeking approval from others, or feeling uncertain about who you are without external validation. In some cases, the opposite extreme may emerge—overcompensating with ego, defensiveness, or a need to dominate in order to feel secure.

There can also be a disconnection from the body, where a person feels out of touch with their own instincts or unsure how to trust themselves. The deeper issue beneath these patterns is often a forgotten truth: the right to exist as oneself without needing to earn that right.

Healing within the First House begins with reclaiming presence. It involves learning to stand in your own energy, to recognize your own voice, and to trust your own instincts even when they are not validated by others. It is the process of returning to yourself, again and again, until being who you are feels natural rather than frightening.

At its highest expression, the First House offers the gift of authentic presence. This is not about perfection, performance, or having everything figured out. It is about being real. It is about showing up as you are, without unnecessary masks or apologies. There is a quiet power in this kind of presence. It does not need to demand attention because it naturally draws it. People can feel when someone is genuinely themselves, and that authenticity creates connection.

Authentic presence also creates permission. When you allow yourself to be who you are, you make it easier for others to do the same. In this way, the First House is not only about personal identity—it is about setting a tone for how others experience themselves in your presence.

Taking time to reflect on this house can deepen your understanding of where you stand in your relationship with yourself. You might ask: Who am I when I am not trying to meet anyone else's expectations? How comfortable am I with being seen exactly as I am? Where in my life am I holding back from beginning something that feels important? What would change if I trusted my instincts more fully?

These questions are not meant to be answered all at once. The First House is a lifelong unfolding. Identity is not static; it evolves as you move through different experiences and stages of life. What remains constant is the invitation to stay connected to yourself as you grow.

Once the soul begins to recognize itself—once it claims its existence and starts to move with intention—it naturally encounters a new question. After "I am," comes the realization that life requires support. The focus begins to shift from simply being to sustaining that being in a tangible way.

This is where the journey continues into the Second House, where the soul learns about value, resources, and the deeper understanding of what it means to feel secure in both the material and inner world.

CHAPTER 15: THE SECOND HOUSE, THE SOUL & SELF-WORTH

The Discovery of Value

After the soul enters the world through the First House and begins forming its identity, a new question naturally arises:

"What do I have that supports my life?"

The Second House represents the stage where the soul begins to understand value, security, and personal resources.

In the First House we discover who we are.

In the Second House we begin to explore what we possess and what we value.

This house governs the material and energetic foundations that help sustain life. It reflects our relationship with resources, wealth, talents, and the deeper sense of self-worth that shapes how we interact with the physical world.

The Connection to Taurus

The Second House carries energy similar to the zodiac sign Taurus, which represents stability, nourishment, and the enjoyment of life's physical pleasures.

Taurus teaches patience and the importance of building strong foundations. In the same way, the Second House encourages the soul to establish stability through wise use of resources.

This house reminds us that life on Earth requires practical support.

Food, shelter, comfort, and financial security all play important roles in sustaining the body and creating a sense of safety.

However, the Second House is not only about material possessions. It also reflects the deeper emotional relationship we have with value itself.

Material Resources and Prosperity

Traditionally, the Second House is associated with money and financial resources.

Yet astrology views money as more than currency. It represents energy in motion, exchanged between people in order to support life and growth.

Through this house we explore questions such as:

How do we earn resources?
How do we manage and protect what we have?
Do we feel secure in our ability to sustain ourselves?

Some individuals naturally attract financial abundance, while others experience challenges related to income or possessions.

The Second House helps reveal the patterns through which these experiences unfold.

But the deeper lesson of this house lies beyond simple wealth.

It lies in understanding true value.

The Meaning of Self-Worth

At its heart, the Second House reflects our sense of self-worth.

Self-worth is the belief that we are deserving of stability, prosperity, and well-being.

When individuals possess strong self-worth, they tend to make choices that support their long-term security.

They value their time, their talents, and their contributions to the world.

However, when self-worth is weakened, individuals may undervalue themselves or struggle to recognize their abilities.

This can lead to patterns such as:

- accepting less than they deserve
- fearing financial instability
- undervaluing personal talents

The Second House invites us to examine these patterns and rebuild a healthy relationship with our own value.

The Gifts We Possess

Beyond material possessions, the Second House also governs personal talents and abilities.

Every individual carries unique gifts.

These gifts may include practical skills, artistic talents, intellectual abilities, or emotional strengths.

The Second House encourages the soul to recognize these natural resources and cultivate them.

Just as a farmer nurtures the soil to produce a harvest, individuals must nurture their talents in order to bring them into the world.

Often, the abilities that sustain us financially are directly connected to the gifts we develop through patience and dedication.

Security and Stability

Another important theme of the Second House is the search for security.

Security does not simply mean possessing wealth. It means feeling confident that life can be sustained and supported.

Some individuals seek security through financial savings, others through stable careers or family structures.

The Second House reflects the ways we attempt to create stability in our lives.

Yet this house also reminds us that true security ultimately arises from inner confidence and resourcefulness.

When individuals trust their ability to create and manage resources, they become less fearful of change and uncertainty.

The Relationship Between Possession and Attachment

While the Second House encourages the development of resources, it also teaches an important spiritual lesson.

Possessions are tools for supporting life, but they should not define our identity.

When individuals become overly attached to material wealth, they may begin to measure their worth solely through external possessions.

This attachment can lead to fear of loss or excessive focus on accumulation.

The deeper wisdom of the Second House reminds us that resources should serve life, not control it.

Balance is achieved when we appreciate material support while remaining aware that true value comes from within.

The Shadow of the Second House

Like all areas of astrology, the Second House contains both strengths and challenges.

When this house becomes unbalanced, individuals may struggle with issues such as:

- financial insecurity
- over-attachment to possessions
- fear of poverty
- undervaluing personal abilities

In some cases, individuals may accumulate wealth but still feel internally insecure.

In other cases, individuals may avoid pursuing prosperity because they believe they are unworthy of success.

The lesson of the Second House is to develop a balanced relationship with both material and inner value.

The Gift of the Second House

At its highest expression, the Second House represents the realization that abundance begins with self-recognition.

When individuals understand their talents and value their contributions, they naturally create opportunities for stability and prosperity.

The Second House teaches the soul to respect its own resources and to cultivate the gifts it has been given.

Through patience, dedication, and self-awareness, the individual learns how to build a life supported by both inner confidence and practical stability.

Reflection

Consider the resources that support your life today.

Beyond money or possessions, what talents and abilities do you possess that create value in the world?

Do you recognize and appreciate these gifts?

The Second House invites you to explore your relationship with value, both the value you hold and the value you bring to others.

When self-worth is honored, prosperity often follows naturally.

The Journey Continues

With identity established and resources developed, the soul becomes ready for the next stage of experience.

Once security is achieved, curiosity begins to grow.

The individual starts asking new questions:

“What can I learn about the world around me?

CHAPTER 16:
THE THIRD HOUSE, THE AWAKENING OF THE MIND

The Birth of Curiosity

After the soul establishes identity in the First House and learns about value and security in the Second House, a natural impulse begins to emerge.

The soul becomes curious.

It begins by asking questions about the world that surrounds it:

How do things work?
What do other people think?
What can I learn from the experiences around me?

This stage of life is represented by the Third House, the house of communication, learning, and intellectual discovery.

Here, the mind awakens, eager to explore and understand the environment in which it lives.

The Connection to Gemini

The Third House carries an energy closely aligned with the zodiac sign Gemini, the sign of communication and curiosity.

Gemini represents the lively movement of ideas, conversations, and connections between people.

In the same way, the Third House governs the exchange of information that helps individuals develop understanding and awareness.

Through this house, we learn how to think, communicate, and share knowledge.

It reflects the development of the mind as a powerful tool for navigating the world.

Learning Through Experience

The Third House represents the earliest forms of learning.

It governs the experiences that shape our understanding of the world during childhood and adolescence.

These experiences often include:

- early education
- basic communication skills
- interactions with siblings
- relationships with neighbors and classmates
- everyday observations of the surrounding environment

Through these interactions, individuals begin forming ideas about how the world functions.

The Third House reminds us that learning does not only occur in classrooms. Much of our knowledge develops through daily experiences and conversations.

Communication as a Bridge Between Minds

One of the most important functions of the Third House is communication.

Communication allows individuals to share ideas, express emotions, and build relationships.

Language becomes a bridge connecting one mind to another.

Through words, gestures, and written expression, we transmit knowledge across generations.

The Third House governs many forms of communication, including:

- speaking
- writing
- listening
- teaching
- storytelling

These abilities allow human beings to collaborate, innovate, and grow together as a society.

The Role of Curiosity

Curiosity is the driving force behind the Third House.

It encourages individuals to ask questions and explore new perspectives.

Curiosity fuels discovery, learning, and intellectual development.

Without curiosity, the mind would remain stagnant.

But when curiosity is embraced, the world becomes a vast field of exploration.

The Third House teaches us that learning is not a destination but a continuous process.

Every new piece of information expands our understanding of life.

Siblings and Early Relationships

The Third House is also associated with siblings and close childhood companions.

These early relationships often play an important role in shaping communication patterns and social development.

Through interactions with siblings and peers, individuals learn how to:

- cooperate
- compete
- share ideas
- resolve conflicts

These experiences help form the social skills that influence relationships throughout life.

The Third House, therefore, represents the first arena where the mind begins interacting actively with others.

The Everyday Environment

Unlike some houses that focus on large life events, the Third House reflects the everyday environment.

It governs daily routines, local travel, neighborhood connections, and ordinary interactions.

Although these experiences may seem simple, they form the foundation of our understanding of the world.

Small conversations, brief encounters, and daily observations all contribute to the growth of awareness.

The Third House reminds us that wisdom often develops through ordinary experiences repeated over time.

The Power of Thought

Thought itself is one of the most powerful forces in human life.

Our thoughts influence how we interpret experiences, make decisions, and interact with others.

The Third House governs the mental processes that shape these thoughts.

Through reflection and learning, individuals develop the ability to examine ideas critically and communicate them effectively.

When the mind is trained with care and curiosity, it becomes a powerful instrument for understanding the world.

The Shadow of the Third House

Like every part of the astrological chart, the Third House also carries potential challenges.

When the energy of this house becomes unbalanced, individuals may struggle with:

- scattered thinking
- superficial understanding
- gossip or miscommunication
- restlessness and lack of focus

Because the Third House thrives on information, it can sometimes become overwhelmed by too many ideas at once.

The lesson of this house is to develop clarity and thoughtful communication rather than constant mental noise.

The Gift of the Third House

At its highest expression, the Third House represents the joy of learning and the power of shared knowledge.

It reminds us that curiosity is one of the greatest gifts of human consciousness.

Through communication, individuals build bridges of understanding between cultures, communities, and generations.

The Third House teaches the soul how to explore the world with an open mind and to share discoveries with others.

In doing so, the mind becomes not only a tool for personal growth but also a vehicle for collective progress.

Reflection

Consider the role communication plays in your life.

How do you share your thoughts and ideas with others?

Are there areas where you feel inspired to learn more or express yourself more clearly?

The Third House invites you to cultivate curiosity and to recognize the power of words and ideas in shaping your experience of the world.

The Journey Continues

With the mind awakened and curiosity engaged, the soul now begins seeking something deeper.

After learning about the outer world through communication and observation, the individual begins turning inward.

A new question arises:

"Where do I truly belong?"

CHAPTER 17: THE FOURTH HOUSE, ROOTS OF THE SOUL

The Foundation of Life

After the mind awakens through the curiosity of the Third House, the soul begins to turn inward and ask a more personal question:

"Where do I belong?"

This question leads us to the Fourth House, the house of home, family, emotional foundations, and the deepest roots of the soul.

While the previous houses focus on identity, value, and learning about the surrounding environment, the Fourth House explores something more intimate.

It represents the inner sanctuary of the heart, the place where we feel safe, protected, and connected to our origins.

This house reminds us that every individual carries an emotional foundation that influences how they move through the world.

The Connection to Cancer

The Fourth House shares a natural connection with the zodiac sign Cancer, the sign of nurturing, protection, and emotional depth.

Cancer energy teaches us the importance of caring for others and creating environments where life can grow and flourish.

Similarly, the Fourth House reflects the environment that nurtures the soul during its earliest stages of development.

It represents the emotional atmosphere in which a person grows, often shaped by family, caregivers, and the home environment during childhood.

These early experiences become the emotional soil from which the individual's identity and relationships later develop.

The Meaning of Home

Home is one of the central themes of the Fourth House.

However, home is not simply a physical building.

Home represents a feeling of safety and belonging.

For some individuals, home may be strongly connected to family traditions and childhood memories. For others, home may become a place they create later in life through meaningful relationships and personal choices.

The Fourth House encourages us to explore what truly gives us a sense of comfort and emotional grounding.

It reminds us that every soul needs a place, whether physical or emotional, where it can rest and renew its strength.

Family and Ancestral Influence

The Fourth House is strongly connected to family roots and ancestry.

Each person is born into a lineage that carries stories, traditions, and emotional patterns passed down through generations.

These inherited influences may shape our beliefs, behaviors, and emotional responses in subtle ways.

The Fourth House invites us to explore these connections.

By understanding our family history, we gain insight into the forces that have shaped our emotional foundation.

Some traditions may provide strength and guidance, while others may reveal patterns that need healing or transformation.

Through awareness, individuals can honor their roots while consciously shaping their own path forward.

Emotional Security

Another key theme of the Fourth House is emotional security.

While the Second House focuses on material security, the Fourth House reflects the deeper sense of emotional stability that allows individuals to feel safe and supported.

This security may come from loving relationships, a peaceful home environment, or the presence of trusted companions.

When emotional security is strong, individuals often feel confident exploring the world and pursuing their goals.

However, when emotional foundations are unstable, individuals may struggle with feelings of uncertainty or disconnection.

The Fourth House reminds us that nurturing emotional well-being is just as important as achieving external success.

The Inner World

The Fourth House also governs the private inner life of the soul.

While the Tenth House represents public reputation and career, the Fourth House represents the personal space where individuals retreat from the outer world.

Here we reflect, dream, and reconnect with our deeper feelings.

This inner world may include:

- personal memories
- emotional reflections
- quiet moments of solitude
- spiritual contemplation

These experiences allow the soul to restore balance and maintain emotional health.

The Fourth House teaches us the importance of honoring our inner lives, not just our outward accomplishments.

The Past and Personal History

The Fourth House is closely tied to the past.

Our childhood experiences, family dynamics, and early emotional impressions often influence the way we approach life as adults.

These memories form the emotional foundation upon which our personality develops.

However, the Fourth House does not trap us in the past.

Instead, it invites us to understand the past so that we can grow beyond its limitations.

When individuals recognize how their early experiences shaped them, they gain the ability to consciously transform those patterns.

Through reflection and healing, the past becomes a source of wisdom rather than restriction.

The Shadow of the Fourth House

Like every part of the astrological chart, the Fourth House carries potential challenges.

When the energy of this house becomes unbalanced, individuals may experience:

- emotional dependency
- difficulty letting go of the past
- family conflicts
- feelings of insecurity or isolation

Sometimes people cling to familiar emotional patterns even when those patterns no longer serve their growth.

The lesson of the Fourth House is to honor our roots while continuing to evolve.

Emotional security should support growth, not prevent it.

The Gift of the Fourth House

At its highest expression, the Fourth House represents the sacred foundation of the soul.

It teaches us that strength does not only come from outward achievements but also from inner stability and emotional understanding.

When individuals nurture their emotional foundations, they develop resilience and compassion.

They create homes, both physical and emotional, where life can flourish.

The Fourth House reminds us that every soul needs a place of belonging, a sanctuary where love and understanding provide the foundation for growth.

Reflection

Consider the places and relationships that give you a sense of home.

What experiences have shaped your emotional foundations?

How can you create environments that nurture both yourself and those around you?

The Fourth House invites you to honor your roots while building a life that reflects your deepest sense of belonging.

The Journey Continues

With emotional foundations established, the soul begins to rediscover the joy of personal expression.

After learning where it belongs, the individual naturally begins asking another question:

“How can I express the creativity and joy within me?

CHAPTER 18:
THE FIFTH HOUSE, THE CREATIVE FLAME OF THE SOUL

The Awakening of Joy

After establishing emotional roots in the Fourth House, the soul begins to feel a natural stirring within itself. Security has been found, the foundation has been built, and now a new question arises from deep within:

"How can I express the life that lives inside me?"

This question opens the doorway to the Fifth House, the house of creativity, self-expression, passion, and the joyful celebration of being alive.

The Fifth House is where the soul begins to shine.

It is where individuality takes on color, form, and movement. In this house, life is not simply lived, it is performed, celebrated, and expressed.

The energy of the Fifth House invites us to rediscover the wonder that exists within the human spirit.

The Connection to Leo

The Fifth House shares a natural resonance with the zodiac sign Leo, the sign of radiance, courage, and creative vitality.

Leo is symbolized by the lion, a creature known for its strength and regal presence. But beneath this powerful symbol lies a deeper spiritual message: the courage to express one's authentic self.

Just as the lion stands proudly in the sunlight, Leo energy encourages individuals to step forward and allow their unique gifts to shine.

In the same way, the Fifth House asks each soul to embrace its creative nature without fear or hesitation.

It teaches that creativity is not limited to artists, musicians, or performers.

Creativity is the life force itself.

Every idea, every expression of love, every moment of laughter is an act of creation.

Creativity as a Spiritual Force

Many people associate creativity with artistic talent, but the Fifth House reveals that creativity is much broader.

Creativity is the ability to bring something new into existence.

This can appear in many forms:

- writing and storytelling
- music and artistic expression
- innovation and invention
- playful imagination
- joyful interaction with others

Creativity is also present in the way we shape our lives, solve problems, and bring beauty into the world.

In truth, creativity is a reflection of the universal creative force that brought the universe itself into being.

Through the Fifth House, individuals participate in this ongoing act of creation.

The Courage to Be Seen

The Fifth House is strongly connected to the desire for recognition.

This is not necessarily a desire for fame or public attention, but rather the natural human need to be acknowledged and appreciated for who we truly are.

Every soul carries a unique spark.

The Fifth House encourages us to reveal that spark without apology.

However, this can sometimes feel vulnerable.

To express one's true self requires courage, because creativity exposes the inner world of the soul.

For this reason, the Fifth House often asks individuals to overcome fears of judgment, criticism, or rejection.

When individuals embrace their creative power, they discover that self-expression becomes one of the most fulfilling experiences life has to offer.

The Role of Play and Joy

One of the most beautiful aspects of the Fifth House is its connection to playfulness and joy.

Children naturally embody the energy of the Fifth House.

They create stories, games, and imaginative worlds without concern for rules or expectations.

As adults, many people forget this playful spirit.

Responsibilities and obligations often overshadow the natural joy that once flowed freely during childhood.

The Fifth House reminds us that play is not a distraction from life, it is an essential part of it.

Through play, laughter, and creative exploration, individuals reconnect with their inner vitality.

Joy becomes a source of renewal for the soul.

Romance and the Heart

The Fifth House also governs romantic attraction and matters of the heart.

While the Seventh House later explores committed partnerships, the Fifth House represents the early spark of love, the excitement, passion, and emotional electricity that occurs when two souls recognize one another.

This form of love is playful, adventurous, and often spontaneous.

It carries a sense of discovery and wonder.

Romantic relationships experienced through the Fifth House often awaken powerful creative and emotional energies.

They inspire poetry, music, art, and expressions of deep affection.

The Fifth House teaches us that love is not merely a social structure, it is a creative force that expands the heart.

Children and the Continuation of Life

Another important theme of the Fifth House is the relationship with children.

Children represent the continuation of life and the unfolding of future generations.

Whether through biological children, mentorship, teaching, or guiding younger individuals, the Fifth House reflects the human desire to nurture and encourage the next wave of life.

Children often mirror the creative energy of the Fifth House through their natural curiosity and imagination.

They remind us that life is meant to be experienced with wonder.

Even individuals without children may express this energy through creative projects, teaching, or contributing to the growth of others.

In this way, the Fifth House represents the act of giving life to something that will continue beyond ourselves.

Risk and Adventure

The Fifth House also carries an element of risk and excitement.

Creative expression often requires individuals to step beyond familiar boundaries.

Artists, inventors, and visionaries frequently take risks when introducing new ideas to the world.

The same principle applies to romance and personal creativity.

To express love or share one's creative work requires courage.

Sometimes the outcome is uncertain.

Yet the Fifth House reminds us that without risk, there can be no discovery.

Taking creative risks allows individuals to explore new possibilities and expand their sense of identity.

Life becomes richer when we allow ourselves to experiment, imagine, and try new things.

The Shadow Side of the Fifth House

Like all areas of the chart, the Fifth House contains both strengths and potential challenges.

When its energy becomes unbalanced, individuals may experience:

- excessive need for attention
- dramatic emotional reactions

- creative blocks
- reckless risk-taking
- ego-driven behavior

These patterns can occur when the desire for recognition becomes stronger than the desire for genuine self-expression.

The true lesson of the Fifth House is not to seek admiration, but to express the authentic joy that lives within the soul.

When creativity flows naturally, recognition often follows as a natural result rather than a goal.

The Sacred Fire Within

At its highest level, the Fifth House represents the sacred fire of life itself.

It is the flame of inspiration that burns within every individual.

This fire drives humanity to create music, write stories, build civilizations, and explore the mysteries of the universe.

Without the energy of the Fifth House, life would become mechanical and predictable.

Creativity is what keeps the human spirit alive.

Every person carries a unique creative spark waiting to be expressed.

The Fifth House invites us to honor that spark and allow it to illuminate the world.

Reflection

Think about the ways in which you express your creativity.

What activities bring you joy, excitement, or inspiration?

How often do you allow yourself to play, imagine, and create without judgment?

The Fifth House reminds us that creativity is not a luxury, it is a vital expression of the soul.

When we honor our creative spirit, we reconnect with the joy of being alive.

The Journey Continues

After the soul has discovered the joy of self-expression, it begins to recognize another truth:

Creative energy must eventually be shaped, refined, and organized in order to bring lasting results.

This realization leads us into the next phase of the astrological journey:

CHAPTER 19:
THE SIXTH HOUSE, THE SACRED WORK OF THE SOUL

Turning Inspiration into Purpose

The Fifth House celebrates creativity and joyful expression. It encourages us to play, imagine, and reveal the spark of life within.

Yet every creative force eventually reaches a moment where it must ask:

"How can this gift serve a purpose?"

This question brings us to the Sixth House, the house of work, discipline, health, responsibility, and meaningful service.

Here, the soul learns an important lesson: inspiration must be supported by effort, patience, and daily commitment.

The Sixth House transforms raw potential into practical reality.

The Connection to Virgo

The Sixth House shares a natural connection with the zodiac sign Virgo, the sign of refinement, analysis, and thoughtful service.

Virgo energy is often misunderstood as being overly focused on details, but its deeper purpose is far more profound.

Virgo represents the desire to improve life through careful attention and dedicated effort.

Just as a gardener carefully tends to plants so that they may grow stronger, Virgo energy works to refine and strengthen the systems that support life.

Through the Sixth House, individuals learn the value of developing their abilities with patience and dedication.

The Meaning of Work

The Sixth House governs the concept of work, but work in this context carries a deeper meaning than simply earning a living.

Work represents the way individuals apply their talents in service to the world.

Every person possesses unique abilities, and the Sixth House asks how these abilities can contribute to the greater good.

Work may appear in many forms:

- professional careers
- craftsmanship and skilled labor
- healing professions
- teaching and mentorship
- service-oriented roles

What matters most is not the title of the job, but the spirit in which the work is performed.

When individuals feel that their efforts contribute meaningfully to life, work becomes a source of satisfaction and pride.

The Value of Discipline

One of the central teachings of the Sixth House is the importance of discipline.

While creativity flows freely in the Fifth House, the Sixth House reminds us that lasting accomplishments require consistent effort.

Musicians practice scales for years before mastering their instruments.

Writers refine their words through repeated revision.

Athletes strengthen their bodies through daily training.

Discipline allows inspiration to take shape.

It transforms dreams into skills and ideas into achievements.

Rather than restricting creativity, discipline gives it structure and strength.

The Art of Improvement

The Sixth House also governs the desire for self-improvement.

Virgo energy naturally seeks to refine and perfect whatever it touches.

This does not mean striving for impossible perfection.

Instead, it reflects the natural human desire to grow, learn, and improve over time.

In this house, individuals often develop the ability to analyze their work carefully, noticing areas that can be strengthened or clarified.

Through this process of refinement, talents become sharper and more effective.

Progress occurs not through sudden leaps, but through steady dedication.

Health and Well-Being

Another major theme of the Sixth House is health and physical well-being.

Because this house governs daily routines and habits, it reflects the practices that support or weaken the body's vitality.

Healthy routines might include:

- balanced nutrition
- regular physical activity

- sufficient rest
- mindful daily habits

When these routines are maintained, the body becomes a strong vessel capable of supporting the soul's work.

The Sixth House reminds us that caring for the body is not simply a personal responsibility, it is part of honoring the life that has been given to us.

Service to Others

Perhaps the most profound aspect of the Sixth House is its connection to service.

Service is often misunderstood as self-sacrifice or submission, but its true meaning is far more uplifting.

Service represents the willingness to contribute one's talents for the benefit of others.

Every society depends upon individuals who are willing to perform essential tasks that sustain the community.

Teachers educate future generations.

Doctors heal the sick.

Craftspeople build the structures that shelter families.

Even small acts of kindness and assistance can create powerful ripples throughout the world.

Through service, individuals recognize that their actions are connected to the well-being of others.

The Dignity of Everyday Effort

Unlike the more dramatic houses of creativity or public recognition, the Sixth House often operates quietly.

Its power lies in the dignity of everyday effort.

Great achievements rarely occur through a single moment of brilliance.

Instead, they emerge from countless small actions performed consistently over time.

A garden grows because someone waters it daily.

A book is written because an author returns to the page again and again.

A healthy body develops through steady habits practiced over years.

The Sixth House teaches that ordinary actions can create extraordinary results.

The Shadow of the Sixth House

When the energy of the Sixth House becomes unbalanced, individuals may experience challenges such as:

- excessive perfectionism
- constant worry about small details
- overworking to the point of exhaustion
- self-criticism or feelings of inadequacy

These patterns can arise when the desire for improvement becomes overly harsh or rigid.

True growth requires patience and compassion.

The Sixth House encourages individuals to pursue excellence while also recognizing the value of rest and balance.

The Sacredness of Work

At its highest level, the Sixth House reveals that work itself can become a spiritual practice.

When individuals approach their daily responsibilities with care, dedication, and gratitude, even simple tasks gain deeper meaning.

Preparing a meal, repairing a tool, or completing a project can become acts of mindfulness and intention.

Through this perspective, work is no longer seen as a burden but as a meaningful contribution to life.

Every action becomes an opportunity to bring order, beauty, and improvement into the world.

Reflection

Consider the routines and responsibilities that fill your daily life.

Do they support your health and growth, or do they create unnecessary strain?

What talents do you possess that could serve others in meaningful ways?

The Sixth House invites you to view your daily efforts as part of a larger purpose.

Through discipline and thoughtful service, ordinary actions become pathways to fulfillment.

The Journey Continues

As individuals develop their skills and dedicate themselves to meaningful work, another realization begins to emerge.

Life is not meant to be lived alone.

Human beings are deeply connected through relationships, cooperation, and shared experiences.

CHAPTER 20:
THE SEVENTH HOUSE, THE MIRROR OF THE SOUL

The Meeting of Two Lives

After the discipline and personal development of the Sixth House, the soul begins to recognize something essential about the human experience:

Life becomes richer, deeper, and more meaningful when it is shared.

This realization opens the doorway to the Seventh House, the house of partnerships, relationships, agreements, and the profound mirror that other people hold before us.

While the First House represents the self, the Seventh House represents the other.

Together they form a powerful axis in the astrological chart, an axis that reveals how identity and relationship must find balance.

The Seventh House teaches us that we often discover who we truly are through the people we encounter along our path.

The Connection to Libra

The Seventh House is naturally aligned with the zodiac sign Libra, the sign of harmony, justice, and balanced relationships.

Libra is symbolized by the scales, a powerful image representing balance between two sides.

This symbol reminds us that healthy relationships require fairness, cooperation, and mutual respect.

Libra energy seeks harmony not through control, but through understanding and thoughtful communication.

The Seventh House reflects this same principle. It invites individuals to create relationships based on balance, trust, and shared growth.

The Nature of Partnership

The Seventh House governs many forms of partnership, including:

- marriage and romantic commitment
- business partnerships
- legal agreements
- close friendships
- collaborative efforts

These relationships are often based on mutual agreement, where both individuals contribute something meaningful to the connection.

Partnerships bring together two different perspectives, two different life histories, and two different personalities.

This blending of experiences creates opportunities for growth that would not exist if a person remained alone.

Through partnership, individuals learn the art of compromise, cooperation, and shared responsibility.

Relationships as Mirrors

One of the most fascinating aspects of the Seventh House is the idea that relationships act as mirrors of the soul.

Often, the qualities we admire or struggle with in others reflect something within ourselves.

For example:

A person who values kindness may be drawn to compassionate partners.

Someone who struggles with insecurity may attract relationships that challenge their confidence.

These reflections are not accidents.

The Seventh House reveals that relationships often serve as powerful teachers.

Through the people we love, and sometimes through those who challenge us, we gain insight into our own character.

Relationships reveal strengths, fears, and emotional patterns that might otherwise remain hidden.

The Art of Balance

Because the Seventh House lies directly opposite the First House, it represents the challenge of balancing self and other.

Too much focus on the self can create selfishness or isolation.

Too much focus on others can lead to self-neglect or loss of personal identity.

Healthy relationships require both individuals to maintain their individuality while also supporting the partnership.

The Seventh House teaches that true connection does not mean losing oneself.

Instead, it means standing strong as an individual while building something meaningful together.

Commitment and Agreements

The Seventh House also governs formal agreements and commitments.

Marriage vows, business contracts, and legal partnerships all fall under the influence of this house.

These agreements create structure and stability within relationships.

They establish clear expectations and responsibilities, helping individuals work together toward shared goals.

Commitment allows relationships to grow deeper over time.

Through commitment, individuals learn patience, loyalty, and trust.

Attraction and Complementary Energies

Another fascinating feature of the Seventh House is its connection to attraction.

People are often drawn to partners who possess qualities they themselves lack.

For example:

A spontaneous person may be attracted to someone more structured and organized.

A highly analytical person may be drawn to someone who is emotionally expressive.

These complementary differences can create balance within a relationship.

However, they can also lead to misunderstandings if both individuals are unwilling to appreciate each other's perspectives.

The Seventh House encourages individuals to recognize that differences can strengthen a partnership rather than weaken it.

Conflict and Growth

Not all relationships are smooth or easy.

Conflicts may arise when individuals hold different expectations or emotional needs.

However, the Seventh House teaches that conflict itself is not the problem.

The real issue lies in how conflict is handled.

When individuals approach disagreements with respect and open communication, relationships can grow stronger through the process.

Difficult moments often lead to deeper understanding and renewed commitment.

Through these experiences, relationships evolve into stronger and more resilient bonds.

The Shadow Side of the Seventh House

Like all areas of the astrological chart, the Seventh House carries potential challenges.

When its energy becomes unbalanced, individuals may experience:

- dependency on relationships for self-worth
- fear of commitment
- repeated patterns of unhealthy partnerships
- struggles for power or control

These challenges often arise when individuals rely on relationships to define their identity.

The Seventh House reminds us that strong partnerships occur when two complete individuals come together, rather than when one person depends entirely upon the other.

The Gift of Shared Life

At its highest expression, the Seventh House represents the beauty of shared experience.

Through partnership, individuals learn compassion, patience, and deeper emotional awareness.

They discover that life becomes richer when responsibilities, joys, and dreams are shared with others.

Relationships allow people to celebrate victories together and support one another during difficult times.

Through love, trust, and cooperation, two individuals can create something greater than either could achieve alone.

The Seventh House teaches that connection is not a limitation, it is a source of profound strength and transformation.

Reflection

Think about the relationships that have influenced your life most deeply.

What have these connections taught you about yourself?

Have certain patterns appeared repeatedly in your partnerships?

The Seventh House invites you to see relationships not only as emotional experiences but also as opportunities for self-discovery and growth.

Through understanding these connections, individuals can build relationships that are balanced, respectful, and deeply fulfilling.

The Journey Continues

As relationships deepen and life becomes shared with others, another realization begins to emerge.

Some experiences transform us in ways that go far beyond everyday partnerships.

These experiences involve profound emotional intensity, shared resources, and deep psychological change.

CHAPTER 22:
THE NINTH HOUSE, THE QUEST FOR TRUTH

The Expansion of the Mind

After experiencing the powerful emotional and psychological transformations of the Eighth House, the soul begins to seek something greater than personal survival or emotional understanding.

A deeper question emerges:

What is the meaning of all this?
Why are we here?
What governs the universe?
What truths lie beyond the limits of everyday life?

These questions open the doorway to the Ninth House, the house of wisdom, philosophy, spiritual exploration, and the expansion of human understanding.

Where earlier houses focus on personal development, the Ninth House looks outward and upward, searching for universal truths.

The Connection to Sagittarius

The Ninth House is naturally associated with the zodiac sign Sagittarius, the sign of exploration, vision, and philosophical inquiry.

Sagittarius is symbolized by the archer, a figure aiming an arrow toward the distant sky.

This powerful symbol reflects humanity's eternal quest to reach beyond the immediate world and discover deeper knowledge.

Sagittarius energy is curious, adventurous, and open to new ideas.

It encourages individuals to explore unfamiliar places, cultures, and perspectives in order to broaden their understanding of life.

Through the Ninth House, the soul begins its journey toward wisdom.

The Search for Meaning

Human beings possess a unique ability to reflect on the nature of existence.

Unlike many other creatures, we ask questions about purpose, destiny, and the origin of the universe.

The Ninth House governs this search for meaning.

It encourages individuals to explore:

- philosophy
- religion and spirituality
- ethics and moral principles
- the nature of truth

humanity's place in the universe

Through these explorations, individuals begin to develop belief systems that guide their actions and decisions.

These beliefs may evolve throughout life as new experiences bring greater understanding.

Higher Learning

Another important theme of the Ninth House is higher education and advanced learning.

While the Third House governs basic communication and early learning, the Ninth House represents deeper intellectual pursuits.

These may include:

- university study
- philosophical investigation
- advanced academic research
- spiritual scholarship
- the study of ancient traditions and wisdom teachings

The Ninth House reflects the human desire to move beyond simple facts and seek broader understanding.

Through study and reflection, individuals expand their awareness of the world and their place within it.

Travel and Cultural Discovery

The Ninth House is also strongly associated with long-distance travel and cultural exploration.

Travel offers individuals the opportunity to experience different ways of life and encounter new perspectives.

By visiting unfamiliar places, people discover that their own customs and beliefs are not the only ways of understanding the world.

Travel broadens the mind.

It challenges assumptions and encourages curiosity.

Through these experiences, individuals often gain a deeper appreciation for the diversity of human cultures and traditions.

In this way, travel becomes not only a physical journey but also a journey of the mind and spirit.

Teaching and Sharing Wisdom

As individuals accumulate knowledge and insight, they often feel inspired to share what they have learned with others.

The Ninth House, therefore, governs teaching and the transmission of wisdom.

Teachers, philosophers, spiritual leaders, and scholars frequently embody the energy of this house.

Their role is to help others expand their understanding and explore new ideas.

Teaching can occur in many forms:

- classroom instruction
- writing books and essays
- public speaking
- mentoring students or seekers
- sharing spiritual guidance

Through teaching, wisdom continues to grow and evolve across generations.

Faith and Belief

The Ninth House also governs faith.

Faith does not necessarily refer to a specific religion, but rather to the inner conviction that life has meaning and direction.

Faith provides individuals with a sense of purpose and hope, even during challenging times.

It encourages people to trust that their experiences contribute to a larger unfolding story.

Different individuals express faith in different ways.

Some find it through organized religion.

Others discover it through philosophical study, meditation, or personal reflection.

Regardless of the path chosen, faith often provides the courage needed to explore life's deeper mysteries.

The Challenge of Beliefs

While belief systems can provide guidance, the Ninth House also reminds us that beliefs must remain open to growth and refinement.

When individuals cling rigidly to ideas without questioning them, beliefs can become restrictive rather than enlightening.

Healthy exploration encourages curiosity and humility.

True wisdom recognizes that knowledge is always evolving.

The Ninth House encourages individuals to seek truth with sincerity while remaining open to new perspectives.

The Spirit of Adventure

The Ninth House is also connected to a sense of adventure.

This adventure is not limited to physical travel.

It also includes the courage to explore new ideas and unfamiliar philosophies.

Great thinkers throughout history have expanded human understanding by daring to question existing assumptions.

Scientific discoveries, philosophical movements, and spiritual awakenings often begin when someone asks a new question.

The Ninth House celebrates this spirit of exploration.

It reminds us that learning is a lifelong journey.

The Shadow of the Ninth House

When the energy of the Ninth House becomes unbalanced, certain challenges may arise.

These may include:

- rigid belief systems
- intolerance toward differing viewpoints
- unrealistic idealism
- excessive risk-taking in pursuit of adventure

In such cases, individuals may become overly attached to their own perspectives.

The lesson of the Ninth House is to balance enthusiasm with wisdom.

True exploration requires both curiosity and discernment.

The Gift of Wisdom

At its highest expression, the Ninth House represents the pursuit of true wisdom.

Wisdom differs from knowledge.

Knowledge involves gathering information, while wisdom involves understanding how that information fits into the larger pattern of life.

Through travel, study, and reflection, individuals develop broader perspectives that allow them to see beyond personal concerns.

They begin to recognize the interconnected nature of humanity and the universe.

This understanding brings a sense of peace and purpose.

Reflection

Think about the beliefs and philosophies that guide your life.

Where did these ideas originate?

Have they evolved over time through experience and reflection?

The Ninth House encourages us to remain curious and open to discovery.

The search for truth is not a destination but an ongoing journey.

The Journey Continues

After expanding its understanding of the world through wisdom and exploration, the soul begins to focus on how it can contribute to society on a larger scale.

CHAPTER 23: THE TENTH HOUSE, THE PATH OF DESTINY

The Climb Toward Purpose

After the soul expands its understanding through the Ninth House, life begins to call it toward responsibility and achievement.

Ideas must now be transformed into action.

Beliefs must be demonstrated through real contributions to society.

This is the work of the Tenth House, the house of ambition, leadership, public reputation, and the unfolding of one's destiny.

Where the Fourth House represents our private foundations, the Tenth House represents our public presence in the world.

It shows how individuals step forward to express their abilities and take their place within the larger structure of society.

The Tenth House is often described as the highest point in the astrological chart, symbolizing the peak of personal development and worldly achievement.

The Connection to Capricorn

The Tenth House is naturally associated with the zodiac sign Capricorn, the sign of discipline, responsibility, and long-term accomplishment.

Capricorn is symbolized by the mountain goat, a creature known for its determination and ability to climb steep terrain.

The mountain goat does not rush to the top.

Instead, it moves carefully, step by step, navigating difficult landscapes with patience and persistence.

This symbol perfectly reflects the nature of the Tenth House.

Success rarely appears suddenly.

True achievement develops gradually through effort, perseverance, and dedication to meaningful goals.

The Meaning of Ambition

Ambition is one of the central themes of the Tenth House.

However, ambition in astrology does not simply mean pursuing wealth or status.

At a deeper level, ambition reflects the soul's desire to fulfill its potential.

Every person carries abilities and talents that can influence the world in unique ways.

The Tenth House reveals how individuals strive to develop those abilities and share them with society.

For some, this may involve leadership in business or government.

For others, it may involve creative influence, education, spiritual guidance, or scientific discovery.

What matters most is the desire to make a meaningful contribution.

Public Reputation

Another key element of the Tenth House is public reputation.

As individuals interact with the larger world, their actions shape how others perceive them.

Reputation develops through consistent behavior over time.

It reflects qualities such as:

- integrity
- responsibility
- leadership ability
- reliability
- dedication to one's work

The Tenth House reminds us that reputation is not built through appearances alone.

It grows through authentic commitment to one's responsibilities and values.

When individuals act with integrity, respect and recognition naturally follow.

Authority and Leadership

The Tenth House also governs the concept of authority.

Authority may appear in many forms:

- leadership positions
- professional roles
- community influence
- mentorship and guidance

Some individuals naturally rise into leadership roles because of their ability to organize, inspire, and guide others.

Leadership in astrology is not about domination.

True leadership involves responsibility for the well-being and progress of those who depend on us.

The Tenth House teaches that authority must be balanced with wisdom and humility.

The Role of Responsibility

Responsibility is one of the defining lessons of the Tenth House.

With increased influence comes increased accountability.

Individuals who seek recognition must also be prepared to accept the consequences of their decisions.

Responsibility includes:

- honoring commitments
- maintaining ethical standards
- making decisions that benefit others as well as oneself

Through responsibility, individuals demonstrate maturity and reliability.

These qualities allow them to build lasting achievements that endure over time.

Career and Professional Life

The Tenth House is often associated with career and professional development.

It reflects the path through which individuals apply their skills in the public sphere.

Career choices may evolve throughout life as people discover new interests or opportunities.

The Tenth House does not dictate a single profession.

Instead, it reflects the direction in which a person seeks to express their ambition and purpose.

For some individuals, this may involve business leadership.

Others may pursue artistic careers, scientific research, education, public service, or spiritual guidance.

Each path offers a different way of contributing to society.

Legacy and Influence

One of the most profound themes of the Tenth House is legacy.

Legacy refers to the lasting impact individuals leave behind through their actions, ideas, and achievements.

Every person contributes something to the unfolding story of humanity.

Some legacies are visible in large accomplishments such as inventions, works of art, or social movements.

Others are expressed through quieter influences, teaching, mentorship, compassion, or community leadership.

Regardless of scale, every meaningful contribution shapes the future in some way.

The Tenth House invites individuals to consider the kind of legacy they wish to create.

The Shadow of the Tenth House

When the energy of the Tenth House becomes unbalanced, challenges may arise, such as:

- excessive ambition
- obsession with status or recognition
- fear of failure
- neglect of personal life in pursuit of success

These patterns occur when individuals become focused solely on external achievements rather than inner fulfillment.

True success requires a balance between professional ambition and personal well-being.

The lesson of the Tenth House is not simply to reach the top of the mountain, but to climb with wisdom and integrity.

The Gift of Purpose

At its highest expression, the Tenth House represents the fulfillment of one's life purpose.

Through dedication, responsibility, and thoughtful leadership, individuals can create meaningful contributions that benefit both themselves and the world around them.

This house reminds us that each person carries a unique role in the unfolding story of humanity.

When individuals align their ambitions with their deeper values, their work becomes more than a career; it becomes a calling.

Reflection

Consider the goals and ambitions that guide your life.

What kind of influence do you hope to have on the world?

What legacy would you like to leave for future generations?

The Tenth House encourages us to pursue success not only for personal recognition but also for the positive impact we can create.

Through purposeful action, the soul fulfills its role within the greater human community.

The Journey Continues

After achieving recognition and establishing a place within society, the soul begins to look toward the broader collective.

Success leads to another realization:

Life is not only about individual achievement, but also about contributing to the progress of humanity as a whole.

CHAPTER 24: THE ELEVENTH HOUSE, THE VISION OF THE FUTURE

Beyond Personal Success

The Tenth House teaches us how to achieve success, establish our reputation, and fulfill our responsibilities in the world.

Yet once individuals reach a certain level of accomplishment, a new awareness often emerges.

They begin to ask:

"How can my efforts help others?"

This shift in perspective marks the transition into the Eleventh House, the house of friendship, community, humanitarian ideals, and the collective future of humanity.

While earlier houses focus on personal growth, the Eleventh House expands the soul's awareness toward shared progress and collective evolution.

The Connection to Aquarius

The Eleventh House is naturally associated with the zodiac sign Aquarius, the sign of innovation, vision, and humanitarian ideals.

Aquarius is symbolized by the water bearer, a figure pouring water from a vessel.

This water does not represent ordinary water, it symbolizes knowledge, insight, and wisdom being shared with humanity.

Aquarius energy seeks to uplift society by introducing new ideas that benefit the greater good.

It encourages individuals to look beyond personal ambitions and imagine a future where humanity evolves toward greater understanding and cooperation.

The Power of Friendship

Friendship plays a central role in the Eleventh House.

Unlike family relationships, which are often shaped by birth or obligation, friendships are chosen freely.

This freedom allows individuals to connect with others who share similar interests, values, and aspirations.

Friends provide encouragement, inspiration, and emotional support.

They often help individuals see possibilities that they might not have discovered alone.

In many cases, friendships formed under the influence of the Eleventh House become powerful alliances that lead to shared achievements and meaningful collaborations.

Community and Shared Goals

The Eleventh House also governs groups, organizations, and communities.

These groups may include:

- social movements
- professional organizations
- cultural associations
- charitable groups
- creative collaborations

Through these communities, individuals unite around shared goals.

Working together allows people to accomplish projects that would be impossible for a single person to achieve alone.

Communities also create spaces where ideas can be exchanged, refined, and expanded.

The Eleventh House reminds us that collective effort is one of the most powerful forces for progress in human history.

Vision and Innovation

Another defining feature of the Eleventh House is its connection to visionary thinking.

Individuals influenced by this house often feel inspired to imagine new possibilities for the future.

These visions may include:

- technological innovation
- social reform
- scientific breakthroughs
- artistic revolutions
- new systems of cooperation

Throughout history, many great advancements have begun with individuals who dared to imagine a different future.

The Eleventh House celebrates this spirit of innovation and forward thinking.

It encourages individuals to look beyond current limitations and explore new possibilities.

The Role of Hope

Hope is a powerful emotional force connected to the Eleventh House.

When people believe that the future can improve, they are more willing to work toward change.

Hope inspires creativity, collaboration, and perseverance.

Without hope, progress becomes difficult because individuals lose the motivation to pursue new ideas.

The Eleventh House therefore encourages individuals to cultivate optimism and faith in the potential for positive change.

Even small contributions can help shape a better future.

Dreams and Aspirations

The Eleventh House also reflects long-term dreams and aspirations.

These dreams often extend beyond personal success.

They may involve goals such as:

- helping others achieve opportunity
- improving social systems
- protecting the environment
- expanding knowledge and education
- creating a more peaceful world

These aspirations give individuals a sense of direction and purpose.

When people unite around shared dreams, they create movements capable of transforming society.

The Strength of Diversity

One of the most beautiful aspects of the Eleventh House is its celebration of diversity.

Communities are strengthened when individuals with different backgrounds, talents, and perspectives work together.

Each person brings unique insights and abilities that enrich the group.

Diversity encourages creativity and innovation because it allows multiple viewpoints to interact and inspire new ideas.

The Eleventh House reminds us that progress often emerges from collaboration among individuals who see the world in different ways.

The Shadow of the Eleventh House

Like all areas of the chart, the Eleventh House carries potential challenges.

When its energy becomes unbalanced, individuals may experience:

- feeling disconnected from society
- difficulty finding supportive communities
- unrealistic expectations about the future
- dependence on group approval

Sometimes individuals become so focused on group identity that they lose sight of their own individuality.

The lesson of the Eleventh House is to balance personal authenticity with collective cooperation.

Healthy communities allow individuals to remain true to themselves while working together toward shared goals.

The Gift of Collective Vision

At its highest expression, the Eleventh House represents humanity's shared vision for the future.

It reminds us that progress is not created by isolated individuals but through collaboration and mutual support.

Each person contributes a piece of the larger puzzle.

When individuals share their ideas, talents, and compassion, they help build a world that reflects humanity's highest potential.

The Eleventh House celebrates the idea that together we can create a future filled with greater understanding, creativity, and harmony.

Reflection

Think about the communities and friendships that influence your life.

What dreams or visions do you share with others?

How might your talents contribute to a larger cause that benefits humanity?

The Eleventh House invites us to see ourselves not only as individuals but also as part of a greater collective journey.

Through cooperation and shared vision, we shape the future together.

The Final Stage of the Journey

As the soul contributes to the collective future through the Eleventh House, another realization begins to emerge.

Beyond community, beyond ambition, and beyond social progress lies something even deeper.

There exists a realm of spiritual connection that transcends individual identity and collective achievement.

This leads us to the final stage of the astrological journey:

The Twelfth House, the house of spiritual awakening, inner healing, dreams, and the eternal connection between the soul and the universe.

CHAPTER 25: THE TWELFTH HOUSE, THE OCEAN OF THE SOUL

The Return to the Infinite

The journey through the zodiac is not simply a path of personal development; it is a cycle of the soul's evolution.

Each house represents a stage of experience, from the awakening of identity to the fulfillment of destiny.

By the time the soul reaches the Twelfth House, it has traveled through the entire landscape of human life.

It has built identity, formed relationships, discovered creativity, pursued wisdom, and contributed to the world.

Now the soul enters a space of quiet reflection and spiritual awareness.

The Twelfth House represents the mystery beyond ordinary understanding, the realm where the boundaries between the individual and the universe begin to dissolve.

The Connection to Pisces

The Twelfth House is naturally associated with the zodiac sign Pisces, the sign of compassion, intuition, and spiritual transcendence.

Pisces is symbolized by two fish swimming in opposite directions, connected by an invisible thread.

This symbol reflects the dual nature of human existence.

One fish swims toward the physical world of experience and action.

The other moves toward the spiritual realm of dreams, imagination, and divine connection.

The Twelfth House invites individuals to explore this deeper dimension of life.

It reminds us that we are not only physical beings living in a material world, but also spiritual beings connected to something vast and mysterious.

The Subconscious Mind

One of the most important themes of the Twelfth House is the subconscious mind.

Much of human behavior is influenced by thoughts and emotions that operate beneath the surface of conscious awareness.

Memories, dreams, fears, and hidden desires often shape our reactions without our realizing it.

The Twelfth House governs this hidden inner landscape.

Through introspection, meditation, and reflection, individuals can begin to understand these deeper layers of the mind.

This awareness allows old emotional patterns to be healed and transformed.

Dreams and Intuition

Dreams are strongly connected to the Twelfth House.

During sleep, the conscious mind relaxes, allowing the subconscious to communicate through images, symbols, and emotions.

Dreams often reveal insights that are not easily accessible during waking life.

They may offer guidance, warnings, or reflections of unresolved feelings.

Intuition also belongs to this house.

Intuition is the quiet inner voice that provides understanding beyond logical reasoning.

Many individuals experience intuitive moments when they suddenly sense the truth of a situation without needing to analyze it.

The Twelfth House encourages us to listen to these subtle messages.

Compassion and Empathy

The Twelfth House is deeply connected to compassion.

Because this house dissolves the boundaries between individuals, it often brings a heightened awareness of the suffering and struggles of others.

This awareness can inspire acts of kindness, generosity, and service.

Many individuals with strong Twelfth House influences feel drawn toward helping professions such as:

- counseling and psychology
- spiritual guidance
- healing arts
- charitable work

- humanitarian service

Through compassion, individuals recognize that all people share the same fundamental hopes and fears.

This understanding creates a sense of unity that transcends personal differences.

Solitude and Inner Reflection

Unlike many other houses that emphasize action and interaction, the Twelfth House values solitude and quiet reflection.

Periods of solitude allow individuals to reconnect with their inner world.

Artists, writers, philosophers, and spiritual seekers often spend time alone in order to explore their thoughts and imagination.

Solitude is not isolation.

Instead, it provides a space where individuals can listen to the deeper voice of the soul.

Through reflection, people gain clarity and insight that may not be available amid the noise of everyday life.

The Healing of the Past

The Twelfth House also represents the process of healing unresolved emotional wounds.

Many experiences from the past leave lasting impressions on the subconscious mind.

Some memories may involve pain, regret, or feelings that were never fully expressed.

The Twelfth House encourages individuals to gently explore these hidden emotions.

Through understanding and forgiveness, the soul can release burdens that have been carried for years.

Healing allows individuals to move forward with greater peace and freedom.

Spiritual Connection

Perhaps the most profound aspect of the Twelfth House is its connection to spiritual awakening.

In this house, individuals begin to sense their connection to something larger than themselves.

Different traditions describe this connection in various ways:

- divine presence
- universal consciousness
- the higher self
- the soul's eternal nature

Regardless of the language used, the Twelfth House represents the realization that life is part of a vast and interconnected universe.

This realization often brings a deep sense of humility and wonder.

The Shadow of the Twelfth House

Because the Twelfth House deals with hidden emotions and spiritual mysteries, it can sometimes bring challenges such as:

- confusion or uncertainty about direction
- emotional withdrawal
- escapism through unhealthy habits
- difficulty facing painful memories

These challenges arise when individuals attempt to avoid the deeper work of self-understanding.

The lesson of the Twelfth House is not to escape reality but to approach it with compassion and awareness.

By confronting hidden fears and emotions, individuals can transform confusion into wisdom.

The Gift of Unity

At its highest expression, the Twelfth House reveals a powerful truth:

We are all connected.

The boundaries that appear to separate individuals are often illusions created by limited perception.

Beneath these boundaries lies a shared human experience.

Through compassion, understanding, and spiritual awareness, individuals recognize their connection to all living beings.

This realization brings a sense of peace that transcends personal struggles.

Reflection

Consider the moments when you have felt deeply connected to something greater than yourself.

Perhaps it occurred through nature, music, meditation, prayer, or acts of compassion.

These experiences reflect the energy of the Twelfth House.

They remind us that life contains mysteries that cannot always be explained through logic alone.

The Twelfth House invites us to embrace these mysteries with humility and curiosity.

The Completion of the Cycle

The Twelfth House completes the journey through the zodiac.

Yet endings in astrology are never truly final.

From the quiet reflection of the Twelfth House, a new spark of awareness begins to form.

That spark becomes the First House once again, the rebirth of identity and the beginning of a new cycle of experience.

In this way, the zodiac represents the eternal rhythm of life:

Birth
Growth
Transformation
Wisdom
Completion
And renewal.

PART III:

THE SIGNS THROUGH THE HOUSES

CHAPTER 26:
THE SOUL MAP OF THE ZODIAC, WHERE THE SIGNS MEET THE HOUSES

The Living Blueprint of the Soul

The zodiac signs and the twelve houses form the two great frameworks of astrology.

The signs represent different types of energy, distinct ways in which life expresses itself.

The houses represent the areas of life where those energies unfold.

When these two systems combine, they create a unique pattern for every individual.

This pattern becomes a map of the soul's journey.

Just as a musical instrument produces different melodies depending on how it is played, the zodiac signs express themselves differently depending on the house in which they appear.

Understanding this interaction allows us to see how personality, experiences, and life direction develop through the astrological chart.

Signs as Energies

Each zodiac sign carries a specific type of energy.

These energies describe how a person approaches life.

For example:

Aries energy is bold and initiating.
Taurus energy is steady and grounding.
Gemini energy is curious and communicative.
Cancer energy is nurturing and protective.

Leo energy is creative and expressive.
Virgo energy is analytical and refining.
Libra energy seeks balance and harmony.
Scorpio energy dives into depth and transformation.
Sagittarius energy explores truth and meaning.
Capricorn energy builds structure and long-term success.
Aquarius energy innovates and envisions the future.
Pisces energy dissolves boundaries and connects to spirit.

Each of these energies represents a different way that life moves through us.

Houses as Life Arenas

While the signs describe how energy behaves, the houses describe where that energy manifests in life.

The houses are like stages upon which the energies of the signs perform.

For instance:

The First House governs identity.
The Second House governs values and resources.
The Third House governs communication and learning.
The Fourth House governs emotional foundations and home.
The Fifth House governs creativity and joy.
The Sixth House governs work and daily habits.
The Seventh House governs relationships and partnership.
The Eighth House governs transformation and shared power.
The Ninth House governs wisdom and exploration.
The Tenth House governs destiny and public achievement.
The Eleventh House governs community and future vision.
The Twelfth House governs spiritual awareness and inner healing.

These houses represent the great arenas of human experience.

When Signs Enter Houses

When a zodiac sign occupies a house in a birth chart, its energy begins to influence that particular area of life.

For example:

Aries in the First House creates a personality that is bold, pioneering, and independent.

Aries in the Seventh House may bring strong-willed partners and relationships that challenge the individual to balance independence with cooperation.

The same sign expresses itself very differently depending on where it appears.

This is why astrology cannot rely on sun signs alone.

Two people born under the same sign may live very different lives because their signs express themselves through different houses.

The Dance Between Energy and Experience

Signs and houses create a dynamic interaction between inner nature and external experience.

The sign represents the internal energy.

The house represents the life situation where that energy is expressed.

Imagine a talented musician.

The musician's skill represents the sign.

The stage where the musician performs represents the house.

A musician might play differently in a quiet concert hall than on a lively festival stage.

In the same way, zodiac energies adapt themselves to the life circumstances represented by the houses.

The Role of Planetary Influence

Planets add yet another dimension to this system.

Each planet represents a different psychological function within the human personality.

For example:

The Sun represents identity and vitality.
The Moon represents emotions and inner needs.
Mercury represents thought and communication.
Venus represents love and attraction.
Mars represents action and desire.
Jupiter represents expansion and opportunity.
Saturn represents structure and responsibility.
Uranus represents innovation and awakening.
Neptune represents dreams and spiritual connection.
Pluto represents transformation and rebirth.

When planets move through signs and houses, they activate specific energies and experiences.

This interaction creates the rich complexity that makes each astrological chart unique.

The Individual Story

Because every chart contains a different combination of signs, houses, and planetary placements, no two people share exactly the same soul map.

Each person carries a distinct set of potentials, challenges, and opportunities.

Some individuals may have strong creative placements that inspire artistic expression.

Others may have powerful leadership influences that guide them toward public responsibility.

Still others may possess deep spiritual placements that lead them toward healing or wisdom traditions.

The chart does not dictate fate.

Instead, it reveals the landscape through which the soul travels.

Within that landscape, individuals still possess the freedom to make choices and shape their own path.

Growth Through Awareness

Astrology offers a powerful tool for self-understanding.

By studying the interaction between signs and houses, individuals can gain insight into their natural tendencies and life patterns.

This awareness allows people to:

- recognize their strengths
- understand their challenges
- develop their talents
- navigate relationships more wisely
- make conscious choices about their future

When individuals understand their astrological blueprint, they gain the ability to work with their natural energies rather than struggle against them.

The Soul's Unique Expression

Every soul enters life carrying a unique combination of experiences and possibilities.

The zodiac chart reflects this individuality.

Some people express courage and leadership.

Others express compassion and healing.

Still others contribute through innovation, creativity, or wisdom.

Each path holds value.

The universe does not require everyone to follow the same journey.

Instead, the beauty of life lies in the diversity of human expression.

The astrological chart helps illuminate these unique pathways.

Preparing for the Next Exploration

Now that we understand how signs and houses combine to shape the soul's expression, we can begin exploring these combinations in greater depth.

In the next section, we will examine how each zodiac sign behaves when placed in different houses of the chart.

These combinations reveal fascinating insights into personality, relationships, career paths, and spiritual development.

They transform astrology from a general philosophy into a practical guide for understanding individual life patterns.

The Journey Continues

The next chapters will explore the many ways that zodiac energies express themselves within the houses.

We begin with the pioneering energy of Aries.

From there we will move through each of the twelve signs, revealing how their energies unfold across the different arenas of life.

This exploration will open a new level of understanding about the intricate design of the astrological chart.

CHAPTER 27: ARIES THROUGH THE HOUSES, THE PATH OF COURAGE

The Spirit of Aries

Aries is the first sign of the zodiac, and with it comes the spark of initiation, courage, and bold movement forward.

Symbolized by the ram, Aries energy pushes through obstacles with determination and fearless curiosity. It represents the moment when life says, *"Let us begin."*

Aries is ruled by Mars, the planet of action, drive, and motivation. This energy encourages individuals to take risks, assert themselves, and explore life with enthusiasm.

Wherever Aries appears in the chart, there is a powerful urge to lead, initiate, and move boldly into new territory.

However, Aries energy can also bring impatience or impulsiveness if it is not balanced with reflection and wisdom.

When placed in different houses of the chart, Aries influences different areas of life with its courageous and pioneering spirit.

Let us now explore how Aries expresses itself throughout the twelve houses.

Aries in the First House

The Pioneer of Identity

When Aries occupies the First House, its energy feels completely at home.

Individuals with this placement often possess strong personalities and natural leadership qualities. They are usually energetic, independent, and confident in expressing themselves.

These individuals often feel compelled to take initiative in life. They rarely wait for others to create opportunities; they prefer to act first and figure things out along the way.

While this placement can produce great courage and charisma, it also requires learning patience and considering the perspectives of others.

Aries in the Second House

The Warrior of Values

With Aries in the Second House, individuals approach finances and personal values with determination and independence.

They often prefer to earn their own resources rather than rely on others. Their financial journey may involve bold ventures or entrepreneurial pursuits.

Money may come through initiative, leadership, or creative risk-taking.

However, this placement may also bring impulsive spending if the individual acts without careful planning.

The lesson here is learning to combine Aries courage with a thoughtful financial strategy.

Aries in the Third House

The Bold Communicator

When Aries appears in the Third House, communication becomes direct, energetic, and passionate.

These individuals often speak with confidence and enthusiasm. They enjoy lively conversations and may be quick thinkers who respond rapidly to ideas and discussions.

Their curiosity pushes them to explore many topics, though they may sometimes move so quickly that they overlook deeper details.

This placement encourages learning how to balance enthusiasm with careful listening.

Aries in the Fourth House

The Protector of Home

With Aries in the Fourth House, strong emotions and protective instincts often shape family life.

These individuals may feel a deep desire to defend and support their loved ones.

They may also prefer independence within their home environment, sometimes creating their own path separate from family expectations.

This placement can bring courage in facing family challenges, but it may also require learning emotional patience and sensitivity.

Aries in the Fifth House

The Creative Flame

Aries in the Fifth House brings powerful creative energy.

These individuals often express themselves through art, performance, sports, or adventurous activities.

They may enjoy being the center of attention and often approach romance with enthusiasm and passion.

Their creativity tends to be spontaneous and bold.

The challenge here is learning to sustain creative projects over time rather than losing interest after the initial excitement fades.

Aries in the Sixth House

The Energetic Worker

When Aries influences the Sixth House, daily work and routines are approached with strong motivation.

These individuals often enjoy active environments where they can move, solve problems, and take initiative.

They may excel in careers that require leadership, physical energy, or quick decision-making.

However, they must also be mindful of stress and burnout, as Aries energy can push individuals to overwork themselves.

Developing balanced routines becomes an important lesson.

Aries in the Seventh House

The Dynamic Partner

With Aries in the Seventh House, relationships often involve strong personalities and passionate interactions.

These individuals may attract partners who are confident, assertive, or adventurous.

Partnerships may feel exciting and dynamic, but conflicts can arise if both partners attempt to dominate the relationship.

The lesson here involves learning cooperation and mutual respect.

When balanced, this placement can create partnerships filled with enthusiasm and shared adventure.

Aries in the Eighth House

The Courage to Transform

Aries in the Eighth House brings bold energy into the realm of transformation and emotional depth.

These individuals may face intense life experiences that require courage and resilience.

They are often unafraid to confront difficult truths about themselves and others.

Financial partnerships and shared resources may involve risk-taking or bold decisions.

This placement encourages using Aries strength to navigate life's deeper mysteries with wisdom.

Aries in the Ninth House

The Adventurous Explorer

When Aries appears in the Ninth House, individuals often pursue knowledge and exploration with enthusiasm.

They may be drawn to travel, philosophical study, or spiritual discovery.

These individuals enjoy exploring new cultures and ideas.

Their beliefs may evolve through direct experience rather than abstract theory.

The challenge is learning patience in the pursuit of wisdom, as deeper understanding often requires time and reflection.

Aries in the Tenth House

The Fearless Achiever

Aries in the Tenth House often produces strong ambition and leadership in professional life.

These individuals may feel called to lead organizations, start businesses, or pursue careers that allow them to take initiative.

They often thrive in environments where independence and bold decision-making are valued.

However, they must also balance ambition with responsibility and ethical leadership.

When guided by integrity, this placement can produce inspiring leaders.

Aries in the Eleventh House

The Visionary Innovator

When Aries energy enters the Eleventh House, individuals often take leadership roles within communities or social movements.

They may be passionate about causes that aim to improve society.

Their ideas for the future are often bold and unconventional.

They may enjoy collaborating with groups while still maintaining their independent perspective.

The challenge is learning patience when working with others who move at a slower pace.

Aries in the Twelfth House

The Spiritual Warrior

Aries in the Twelfth House creates a unique combination of courage and spiritual depth.

These individuals may feel driven to confront inner fears and explore the hidden dimensions of the mind.

They may possess strong intuitive abilities and a desire to understand the subconscious world.

At times, they may struggle with inner restlessness or unresolved emotions.

However, when they channel Aries courage inward, they can become powerful agents of healing and spiritual transformation.

Reflection

Aries represents the spark of life itself, the impulse that begins every journey.

When this fiery energy moves through different houses of the chart, it influences various aspects of life with courage, enthusiasm, and determination.

By understanding where Aries appears in the chart, individuals can learn where they are most likely to feel driven to take initiative and pursue new experiences.

The key lesson of Aries is simple but powerful:

Life rewards those who have the courage to begin.

CHAPTER 28:
TAURUS THROUGH THE HOUSES, THE PATH OF STABILITY

The Spirit of Taurus

After the bold spark of Aries begins the cycle of life, the universe introduces a second force, one that slows the pace and asks us to build something lasting.

This is the energy of **Taurus**, the second sign of the zodiac.

Taurus is symbolized by **the bull**, a creature known for its strength, patience, and quiet determination. Unlike Aries, which rushes forward, Taurus stands firmly upon the earth. It values stability, comfort, beauty, and the cultivation of resources that sustain life.

Taurus is ruled by **Venus**, the planet of love, harmony, and beauty. Because of this influence, Taurus energy often seeks experiences that nourish the senses and create a feeling of security.

Where Aries begins the journey, Taurus teaches us how to **sustain and protect what has been created**.

When Taurus appears in different houses of the chart, its steady and grounding influence shapes those areas of life in meaningful ways.

Taurus in the First House

The Steady Presence

When Taurus occupies the First House, individuals often possess a calm and grounded personality. Their presence may feel steady and reassuring to others.

They typically approach life with patience rather than impulsiveness. Decisions are made carefully, and once a path is chosen, they tend to remain committed to it.

This placement often brings physical endurance and a natural appreciation for beauty, comfort, and quality.

However, the lesson here is learning flexibility, since Taurus energy can sometimes resist change even when growth requires it.

Taurus in the Second House

The Builder of Wealth

The Second House is naturally aligned with Taurus energy, so this placement feels particularly strong.

Individuals with Taurus in the Second House often have a natural ability to accumulate resources and create financial stability.

They value security and may work diligently to build lasting wealth or possessions that reflect quality and craftsmanship.

Their approach to money tends to be practical and patient.

However, they must guard against becoming overly attached to material possessions, remembering that true value also lies in experiences and relationships.

Taurus in the Third House

The Thoughtful Communicator

With Taurus in the Third House, communication becomes steady, thoughtful, and deliberate.

These individuals may prefer meaningful conversations over fast-paced discussions.

They often express their ideas with calm clarity, and their words may carry weight because they speak carefully rather than impulsively.

Learning may occur at a slower pace, but knowledge gained tends to be deeply understood and long-lasting.

The challenge here is remaining open to new ideas rather than becoming fixed in familiar viewpoints.

Taurus in the Fourth House

The Keeper of Home

When Taurus appears in the Fourth House, home and family often become central sources of comfort and stability.

These individuals may take great pride in creating a peaceful and beautiful home environment.

They often value family traditions and may feel deeply connected to their roots.

Security within the home becomes essential for emotional well-being.

However, they must also learn that emotional growth sometimes requires stepping beyond the familiar patterns of the past.

Taurus in the Fifth House

The Lover of Beauty

Taurus in the Fifth House brings strong creative and romantic energy.

These individuals often appreciate art, music, and other forms of beauty.

Romantic relationships may develop slowly but tend to be loyal and deeply affectionate.

Creativity may express itself through artistic pursuits, craftsmanship, or the enjoyment of sensory experiences such as music and nature.

The lesson here is to remain open to spontaneity, as Taurus energy sometimes prefers comfort over creative risk.

Taurus in the Sixth House

The Patient Worker

With Taurus influencing the Sixth House, individuals often approach work with dedication and reliability.

They tend to value stable routines and may thrive in careers where consistency and practical skill are appreciated.

Their work ethic is often strong, and they may take pride in mastering their craft.

Health and well-being may benefit from steady habits and balanced lifestyles.

However, they must guard against becoming stuck in routines that limit growth or opportunity.

Taurus in the Seventh House

The Loyal Partner

When Taurus occupies the Seventh House, relationships are approached with seriousness and devotion.

These individuals often seek stable and long-lasting partnerships.

Loyalty and trust become central themes in their relationships.

They may be drawn to partners who provide emotional security and reliability.

However, this placement can sometimes bring possessiveness if individuals become overly attached.

The lesson is to balance loyalty with mutual independence.

Taurus in the Eighth House

The Guardian of Shared Resources

Taurus in the Eighth House creates a strong focus on financial partnerships and shared resources.

These individuals may approach investments or joint finances with caution and careful planning.

Emotionally, they may value deep loyalty in intimate relationships and may take time to trust others fully.

This placement encourages individuals to balance Taurus stability with the transformative energy of the Eighth House.

Learning to embrace change becomes an important part of personal growth.

Taurus in the Ninth House

The Seeker of Practical Wisdom

When Taurus appears in the Ninth House, individuals may pursue knowledge that has practical value.

Their philosophy of life often emphasizes stability, patience, and appreciation for the natural world.

Travel may be enjoyed when it offers comfort and opportunities to experience beauty or culture.

These individuals often prefer wisdom that can be applied to everyday life rather than abstract theories.

The challenge here is remaining open to new ideas and unfamiliar perspectives.

Taurus in the Tenth House

The Architect of Success

Taurus in the Tenth House often produces individuals who build success gradually but securely.

Their careers may involve fields connected to finance, art, agriculture, architecture, or any profession that values craftsmanship and long-term results.

They may become respected for their reliability and steady leadership.

Rather than seeking rapid success, they prefer to construct achievements that endure.

Patience becomes their greatest strength in reaching professional goals.

Taurus in the Eleventh House

The Builder of Community

With Taurus in the Eleventh House, friendships and communities often provide stability and lasting support.

These individuals may prefer a small circle of loyal friends rather than large social groups.

Their contributions to society may focus on creating sustainable systems that benefit future generations.

They may also support causes related to nature, environmental protection, or economic stability.

The lesson here is remaining open to change within group dynamics.

Taurus in the Twelfth House

The Quiet Healer

When Taurus appears in the Twelfth House, individuals often find peace through solitude, nature, and spiritual reflection.

They may possess a deep connection to the natural world and may feel restored when surrounded by beauty and tranquility.

This placement can bring hidden artistic talents or intuitive sensitivity.

However, individuals may sometimes hold onto emotional patterns longer than necessary.

Learning to release attachments allows the soul to experience deeper spiritual freedom.

Reflection

Taurus represents the strength to build and sustain life.

Where Aries begins the journey with courage, Taurus ensures that what is created can endure.

By understanding where Taurus appears in the chart, individuals can discover the areas of life where they seek stability, beauty, and lasting value.

The lesson of Taurus is simple yet profound:

What we nurture with patience and care becomes the foundation of our future.

The Journey Continues

After the stability of Taurus comes the lively curiosity of the next sign.

Life now begins to move faster, ideas begin to multiply, and communication becomes the bridge that connects individuals with the world around them.

CHAPTER 29:
GEMINI THROUGH THE HOUSES, THE PATH OF CURIOSITY

The Spirit of Gemini

Gemini is the third sign of the zodiac, and it represents the awakening of the mind.

Symbolized by the twins, Gemini reflects the dual nature of human thought, the ability to see more than one perspective at a time. It reminds us that knowledge is not fixed but constantly evolving through dialogue, learning, and exploration.

Gemini is ruled by Mercury, the planet of communication, intellect, and quick thinking. Because of this influence, Gemini energy thrives on exchanging ideas, gathering information, and connecting people through words and understanding.

Where Taurus stabilizes life, Gemini begins to ask questions about it.

Wherever Gemini appears in the chart, there is an urge to explore, communicate, and understand the world through conversation and curiosity.

Let us now see how Gemini expresses itself through the twelve houses.

Gemini in the First House

The Curious Personality

When Gemini appears in the First House, individuals often present themselves as lively, curious, and mentally active.

They may have quick wit and an engaging way of communicating with others. Their personalities may feel youthful and adaptable.

These individuals often enjoy meeting new people and learning about many subjects.

However, they may sometimes struggle with indecision because they can see multiple sides of every situation.

The lesson here is learning to focus their curiosity into clear direction.

Gemini in the Second House

The Flexible Value System

With Gemini in the Second House, individuals often approach finances and personal resources with flexibility.

They may earn money through communication-based activities such as writing, teaching, speaking, or media work.

Their values may evolve over time as they gather new knowledge and experiences.

This placement encourages developing financial strategies that allow room for adaptability while maintaining stability.

Gemini in the Third House

The Natural Communicator

Gemini feels especially comfortable in the Third House, which it naturally governs.

Individuals with this placement often possess strong communication skills.

They may enjoy writing, speaking, teaching, or engaging in lively discussions.

Learning is often a lifelong pursuit, and they may explore many different subjects.

However, the challenge is maintaining depth in learning rather than moving too quickly from one topic to another.

Gemini in the Fourth House

The Storyteller of Home

When Gemini appears in the Fourth House, the home environment may be filled with conversation, ideas, and learning.

These individuals may enjoy discussing family history, storytelling, or preserving memories through writing or communication.

Their emotional life may be closely connected to intellectual understanding.

However, they may sometimes analyze feelings rather than experiencing them fully.

Learning emotional expression becomes an important part of growth.

Gemini in the Fifth House

The Playful Creator

Gemini in the Fifth House brings lively creativity and playful expression.

These individuals may enjoy artistic activities that involve communication, such as writing stories, performing, or creating educational entertainment.

Romantic relationships may begin through intellectual attraction and shared conversation.

The challenge here is learning to focus creative energy on completing projects rather than starting many ideas at once.

Gemini in the Sixth House

The Analytical Worker

With Gemini in the Sixth House, individuals often bring mental agility to their work environment.

They may thrive in careers that involve problem-solving, communication, data analysis, or teaching.

Their daily routines may include constant learning or interaction with others.

However, mental overstimulation can sometimes lead to stress.

Balancing mental activity with relaxation becomes important for maintaining well-being.

Gemini in the Seventh House

The Communicative Partner

When Gemini influences the Seventh House, relationships often revolve around conversation and intellectual connection.

These individuals may be drawn to partners who stimulate their minds and share their curiosity about the world.

Partnerships often flourish when communication remains open and lively.

However, relationships may struggle if communication becomes superficial or inconsistent.

The lesson here is cultivating both intellectual and emotional depth within partnerships.

Gemini in the Eighth House

The Investigator of Mysteries

Gemini in the Eighth House brings intellectual curiosity into the realm of transformation and deep emotional experiences.

These individuals may enjoy studying psychology, hidden knowledge, or complex financial systems.

They may feel drawn to uncover mysteries or explore the deeper workings of the human mind.

The challenge here is learning to balance intellectual curiosity with emotional sensitivity.

Gemini in the Ninth House

The Seeker of Knowledge

When Gemini appears in the Ninth House, individuals often feel drawn to explore many different philosophies, cultures, and belief systems.

They may enjoy travel, writing, teaching, or studying languages.

Their worldview often evolves through exposure to diverse ideas.

The lesson is learning to integrate knowledge into a coherent philosophy rather than constantly shifting beliefs.

Gemini in the Tenth House

The Public Speaker

Gemini in the Tenth House often brings careers connected to communication.

These individuals may become writers, journalists, teachers, broadcasters, or public speakers.

Their professional reputation may be built on their ability to explain ideas clearly and connect with audiences.

They may experience multiple career paths throughout life as their interests evolve.

Adaptability becomes one of their greatest strengths.

Gemini in the Eleventh House

The Social Connector

When Gemini appears in the Eleventh House, individuals often enjoy large social networks and communities centered around shared ideas.

They may thrive in organizations that promote communication, education, or technological advancement.

Friendships often develop through intellectual exchange and collaborative thinking.

The challenge here is maintaining deep connections rather than spreading attention too widely across many acquaintances.

Gemini in the Twelfth House

The Intuitive Thinker

Gemini in the Twelfth House creates a fascinating blend of intellect and intuition.

These individuals may experience vivid dreams or possess strong imaginative abilities.

Their minds may often explore hidden psychological or spiritual questions.

Writing, meditation, or quiet reflection may help them express their inner thoughts.

The lesson here is trusting intuition while balancing it with clear communication.

Reflection

Gemini represents the joy of learning and the power of communication.

It reminds us that knowledge grows through curiosity and conversation.

Where Gemini appears in the chart reveals where individuals feel inspired to ask questions, gather information, and connect ideas.

The lesson of Gemini is simple yet profound:

Understanding grows when we remain curious.

The Journey Continues

After the lively exchange of ideas through Gemini, the zodiac journey moves toward a deeper emotional experience.

CHAPTER 30: CANCER THROUGH THE HOUSES, THE PATH OF THE HEART

The Spirit of Cancer

Cancer is the fourth sign of the zodiac and represents the awakening of emotional awareness and the need for belonging.

Symbolized by the crab, Cancer carries its home wherever it goes. The crab's protective shell reflects the emotional sensitivity of this sign. Beneath that shell lies a deeply caring nature that seeks to protect and nurture the people and environments it loves.

Cancer is ruled by the Moon, the celestial body that governs emotional rhythms, intuition, and cycles of change. Just as the Moon moves through phases, Cancer energy often reflects the changing tides of human feeling.

Where Cancer appears in the chart, individuals seek emotional security, connection, and a sense of home.

Cancer reminds us that while the mind may explore the world, the heart longs for roots.

Let us explore how this nurturing energy unfolds through the houses of life.

Cancer in the First House

The Empathic Presence

When Cancer appears in the First House, individuals often project warmth, sensitivity, and emotional awareness.

They may instinctively sense the feelings of others and respond with compassion.

These individuals often appear gentle or protective, and others may naturally turn to them for comfort.

However, their emotional openness can sometimes make them vulnerable to the moods of their surroundings.

Learning emotional boundaries becomes an important life lesson.

Cancer in the Second House

The Guardian of Security

With Cancer in the Second House, individuals often associate security with emotional stability.

Financial decisions may be influenced by the desire to protect family or create a safe home environment.

They may value possessions that hold sentimental meaning rather than purely material worth.

This placement encourages building resources that support both emotional and financial stability.

Cancer in the Third House

The Emotional Communicator

Cancer in the Third House brings emotional sensitivity into communication.

These individuals often speak with warmth and empathy, and their words may comfort others.

They may enjoy storytelling, journaling, or sharing family memories.

Communication with siblings or close relatives may hold special importance.

The challenge is learning to express emotions clearly rather than retreating into silence when feelings become overwhelming.

Cancer in the Fourth House

The Keeper of Roots

Cancer feels naturally aligned with the Fourth House, which governs home and family.

Individuals with this placement often feel a strong connection to their family heritage and emotional foundations.

Creating a nurturing home environment becomes deeply important.

They may enjoy preserving traditions, cooking for loved ones, or maintaining family bonds.

However, they must also learn that growth sometimes requires stepping beyond familiar comforts.

Cancer in the Fifth House

The Loving Creator

When Cancer appears in the Fifth House, creativity often carries emotional depth.

These individuals may express themselves through art, storytelling, music, or nurturing children.

Romantic relationships may feel deeply emotional and protective.

They often seek meaningful emotional connections rather than casual encounters.

This placement encourages balancing emotional investment with personal independence.

Cancer in the Sixth House

The Compassionate Helper

Cancer in the Sixth House often brings nurturing energy into daily work and service.

These individuals may feel drawn to helping professions such as caregiving, healthcare, teaching, or counseling.

They often care deeply about the well-being of those around them.

Work environments that feel supportive and emotionally safe are important for their success.

The lesson here involves learning to care for others without neglecting their own needs.

Cancer in the Seventh House

The Devoted Partner

When Cancer appears in the Seventh House, relationships often become deeply emotional and protective.

These individuals seek partners who offer warmth, loyalty, and emotional understanding.

Marriage and long-term partnerships may feel like a sacred commitment.

However, they must guard against becoming overly dependent on relationships for emotional security.

True partnership requires both connection and personal strength.

Cancer in the Eighth House

The Emotional Transformer

Cancer in the Eighth House brings deep emotional intensity into the realm of transformation.

These individuals may experience profound emotional bonds with others.

They may possess strong intuition and sensitivity toward hidden emotional dynamics.

Shared resources and financial partnerships may carry emotional significance.

Learning to trust their instincts while maintaining emotional balance becomes an important life lesson.

Cancer in the Ninth House

The Seeker of Spiritual Belonging

When Cancer appears in the Ninth House, individuals often seek emotional meaning within their belief systems.

Their spiritual or philosophical views may feel deeply personal and connected to family traditions.

Travel may be experienced as a search for emotional understanding rather than simply adventure.

They often look for wisdom that provides comfort and guidance for the heart.

Cancer in the Tenth House

The Nurturing Leader

Cancer in the Tenth House often produces leaders who guide with empathy and emotional awareness.

Their careers may involve roles where caring for others becomes central.

They may be respected for their compassion and ability to support those around them.

However, they must learn to balance emotional sensitivity with professional objectivity.

When balanced, this placement creates leadership rooted in genuine care.

Cancer in the Eleventh House

The Protector of Community

With Cancer in the Eleventh House, friendships often feel like extended family.

These individuals may create strong emotional bonds within their social circles.

They often support community causes that focus on protection, nurturing, or social welfare.

Their friendships may be loyal and long-lasting.

The challenge is learning to remain open to new connections while maintaining emotional balance.

Cancer in the Twelfth House

The Spiritual Caregiver

Cancer in the Twelfth House creates deep emotional and spiritual sensitivity.

These individuals may possess strong intuitive or psychic awareness.

They often feel drawn toward helping others in quiet or private ways.

Meditation, reflection, or creative expression may help them process their emotions.

Their greatest strength lies in their ability to bring healing and compassion to those in need.

Reflection

Cancer represents the sacred importance of emotional connection and belonging.

Where Aries acts and Gemini thinks, Cancer feels.

It teaches us that life is not only about achievement or knowledge, it is also about nurturing the bonds that sustain us.

Where Cancer appears in the chart reveals where individuals seek emotional security and where they are called to offer care and protection.

The lesson of Cancer is gentle yet powerful:

The heart is strongest when it learns both to protect and to trust.

The Journey Continues

After Cancer nurtures the emotional roots of life, the zodiac cycle moves toward the radiant expression of personal creativity and confidence.

CHAPTER 31:
LEO THROUGH THE HOUSES, THE PATH OF RADIANCE

The Spirit of Leo

Leo is the fifth sign of the zodiac and represents creative expression, courage, and the joyful celebration of life.

Symbolized by the lion, Leo carries a natural sense of dignity, confidence, and strength. The lion stands proudly in the sunlight, reminding us that every soul carries a unique light meant to be shared with the world.

Leo is ruled by the Sun, the center of our solar system and the source of warmth and vitality. In astrology, the Sun represents identity, life force, and the creative spark that animates the human spirit.

Wherever Leo appears in the chart, there is a desire to express individuality, inspire others, and live life with passion.

Leo teaches that life is not only about survival, it is also about celebrating existence and allowing our inner light to shine.

Let us explore how Leo expresses its radiant energy through the twelve houses.

Leo in the First House

The Natural Leader

When Leo appears in the First House, individuals often possess a strong and charismatic presence.

Their personalities may feel vibrant and expressive, and others may naturally notice their confidence.

They often enjoy leading or inspiring others and may possess natural performance abilities.

However, the lesson of this placement is learning humility and remembering that true leadership comes through generosity and encouragement rather than dominance.

Leo in the Second House

The Proud Creator of Value

With Leo in the Second House, individuals often associate personal value with creativity and self-expression.

They may earn resources through artistic talent, leadership roles, or ventures that allow them to showcase their individuality.

They often take pride in their possessions and may enjoy surrounding themselves with beautiful or luxurious items.

The challenge is learning that true worth comes from inner confidence rather than external validation.

Leo in the Third House

The Dramatic Communicator

Leo in the Third House brings warmth and enthusiasm into communication.

These individuals often speak with confidence and may enjoy storytelling, teaching, or performing.

Their conversations may be lively and expressive, and they often enjoy sharing ideas in ways that captivate others.

However, they must also learn to listen as attentively as they speak.

Leo in the Fourth House

The Proud Guardian of Home

When Leo appears in the Fourth House, individuals often feel a strong desire to create a warm and welcoming home environment.

They may take pride in their family heritage and enjoy hosting gatherings or celebrations.

Their homes often become places of warmth, creativity, and personal expression.

The lesson here is balancing pride in one's roots with openness to emotional growth.

Leo in the Fifth House

The Radiant Creator

Leo feels especially powerful in the Fifth House, which it naturally governs.

Individuals with this placement often possess strong creative talents and a deep love of artistic expression.

They may thrive in performance, art, entertainment, or any activity that allows them to express their individuality.

Romantic relationships may be passionate and dramatic.

The challenge is learning that creativity flows most freely when it comes from joy rather than a need for recognition.

Leo in the Sixth House

The Inspired Worker

With Leo in the Sixth House, individuals often bring creativity and enthusiasm into their daily work.

They may excel in careers where they can inspire others or take leadership roles within their work environment.

Their work often feels most fulfilling when it allows them to express their individuality.

However, they must guard against burnout by remembering that rest and humility are also important parts of growth.

Leo in the Seventh House

The Devoted Partner

When Leo influences the Seventh House, individuals often seek relationships filled with warmth, admiration, and loyalty.

They may be drawn to partners who are confident and expressive.

Relationships often thrive when both partners celebrate one another's strengths.

However, power struggles may occur if one partner seeks constant attention or validation.

True partnership grows through mutual appreciation and respect.

Leo in the Eighth House

The Courageous Transformer

Leo in the Eighth House brings courage into the realm of deep emotional transformation.

These individuals may face powerful experiences that test their inner strength.

They often possess the ability to guide others through emotional or psychological challenges.

Financial partnerships may involve bold decisions or creative strategies.

The lesson here is learning to transform pride into wisdom.

Leo in the Ninth House

The Passionate Philosopher

When Leo appears in the Ninth House, individuals often approach learning and philosophy with enthusiasm.

They may enjoy teaching, public speaking, or sharing their beliefs with others.

Travel may become a source of inspiration and personal growth.

Their belief systems often emphasize personal empowerment and creative expression.

The challenge is remaining open to differing perspectives.

Leo in the Tenth House

The Public Star

Leo in the Tenth House often produces individuals who seek recognition for their achievements.

They may pursue careers that allow them to stand in the spotlight, such as leadership, entertainment, education, or entrepreneurship.

Their ambition is often fueled by a desire to inspire others through their accomplishments.

However, they must balance ambition with humility and ethical leadership.

Leo in the Eleventh House

The Inspirational Friend

With Leo in the Eleventh House, individuals often become leaders within their communities or social groups.

They may inspire others with their creativity and enthusiasm for shared goals.

Friendships may be vibrant and supportive.

They often enjoy working with groups that promote artistic expression or humanitarian causes.

The lesson here is learning collaboration rather than seeking personal recognition within group efforts.

Leo in the Twelfth House

The Hidden Light

Leo in the Twelfth House creates a fascinating combination of creativity and spiritual depth.

These individuals may possess powerful inner imagination or artistic ability that expresses itself in quiet or private ways.

They may feel drawn toward spiritual exploration or creative work that touches the subconscious mind.

Their challenge is overcoming self-doubt and recognizing the brilliance that already exists within them.

Reflection

Leo represents the creative fire of the soul.

It reminds us that every person carries a unique light that deserves to be expressed.

Where Leo appears in the chart reveals where individuals feel inspired to shine, create, and inspire others.

The lesson of Leo is both simple and powerful:

When we express our authentic light, we illuminate the path for others as well.

The Journey Continues

As the cycle comes full circle, the Leo lesson remains like a steady flame at the center of the soul's evolution: you were born to shine, not for applause, but to warm the world with what is true in you.

Throughout this journey, you have met every sign as a teacher, yet Leo reminds you that no wisdom is fully lived until it is expressed. Insight becomes embodied when it is carried with dignity, when the heart stays open, and when creative courage is used in the service of love.

When life returns you to beginnings, new seasons, new relationships, new callings, you may notice the same themes appearing again. This is not repetition, but refinement. Each turn of the spiral asks you to let the ego soften while the inner Sun grows brighter: a self that no longer needs to prove its worth, because it knows its worth.

So the journey continues, through your choices, your healing, your relationships, and your creations. And wherever you go next, carry Leo's highest gift with you: generosity of spirit. Let your light make room for others to shine, and you will discover that the soul's path is not a destination, but an ever-deepening return to the heart.

CHAPTER 32:
VIRGO THROUGH THE HOUSES, THE PATH OF REFINEMENT

The Spirit of Virgo

Virgo is the sixth sign of the zodiac and represents refinement, service, healing, and wisdom gained through careful observation.

Its symbol is the Maiden, a figure that represents purity of intention and the desire to cultivate what is meaningful and useful in life. Unlike other signs that move with bold emotion or dramatic expression, Virgo moves with thoughtful precision.

Virgo is ruled by Mercury, the planet of thought, communication, and understanding. While Mercury in Gemini expresses curiosity and conversation, Mercury in Virgo expresses analysis, discernment, and practical intelligence.

Virgo energy seeks to improve what already exists.

It looks at the world not with criticism, but with a deep awareness of how things can become better, healthier, and more harmonious.

Where Virgo appears in a birth chart, we find the areas of life where the soul learns patience, mastery, and the quiet art of thoughtful care.

Let us now explore how Virgo expresses itself through each of the twelve houses.

Virgo in the First House

The Thoughtful Observer

When Virgo occupies the First House, individuals often present themselves with calm intelligence and careful awareness.

They may appear modest or reserved at first, yet their minds are constantly observing and processing information about the world around them.

These individuals often strive to improve themselves physically, mentally, and spiritually.

Their challenge is learning that perfection is not required for growth, progress itself is already a form of success.

Virgo in the Second House

The Careful Builder of Resources

With Virgo in the Second House, individuals often approach finances and resources with practical awareness.

They tend to be thoughtful planners who prefer stability and careful budgeting.

These individuals often build security slowly through discipline and effort rather than sudden opportunities.

Their deeper lesson is learning that self-worth cannot be measured only through productivity or material accomplishment.

Virgo in the Third House

The Analytical Communicator

Virgo in the Third House produces individuals with sharp and perceptive minds.

They often excel in writing, research, teaching, or any activity that involves careful analysis of information.

Their communication style may be precise and thoughtful.

They often notice details that others overlook.

The challenge for this placement is avoiding excessive self-criticism or overthinking.

Virgo in the Fourth House

The Organizer of Home

When Virgo appears in the Fourth House, individuals often feel a strong need to create order and harmony within the home.

Their living spaces may be thoughtfully arranged, and they may feel responsible for maintaining stability within the family.

These individuals may also become caretakers or problem-solvers for relatives.

Their lesson is remembering that emotional connection matters just as much as practical responsibility.

Virgo in the Fifth House

The Skilled Creator

With Virgo in the Fifth House, creativity often expresses itself through skill and craftsmanship.

These individuals may enjoy activities that require precision, such as writing, music, crafts, or design.

Their artistic abilities often grow through practice and discipline rather than spontaneous inspiration.

Romantic relationships may also be approached thoughtfully.

The challenge here is allowing playfulness and spontaneity to accompany careful skill.

Virgo in the Sixth House

The Natural Healer

Virgo feels especially at home in the Sixth House, which it naturally governs.

Individuals with this placement often feel drawn toward healing professions, caregiving roles, or work that improves the well-being of others.

They may be particularly attentive to health, nutrition, and physical balance.

Their ability to notice small changes often makes them effective helpers and guides.

However, they must guard against overwork or worrying too much about perfection.

Virgo in the Seventh House

The Thoughtful Partner

When Virgo influences the Seventh House, individuals often approach relationships with careful consideration.

They may seek partners who share their values of responsibility, honesty, and mutual improvement.

Relationships may feel like partnerships built upon teamwork and shared goals.

However, they must avoid becoming overly critical of themselves or their partners.

Healthy relationships thrive when compassion accompanies discernment.

Virgo in the Eighth House

The Investigator of Hidden Truths

Virgo in the Eighth House brings analytical ability into deep psychological or transformative areas of life.

These individuals may be fascinated by mysteries, psychology, healing sciences, or spiritual research.

They often seek to understand how emotional and energetic patterns shape human behavior.

Financial partnerships may require careful management.

The lesson here is learning to balance analysis with trust in life's deeper mysteries.

Virgo in the Ninth House

The Student of Wisdom

When Virgo occupies the Ninth House, individuals often pursue knowledge with disciplined curiosity.

They may enjoy studying philosophy, science, medicine, or spiritual traditions.

Unlike dramatic belief systems, they often prefer teachings that can be applied in practical ways.

Travel may be approached with a spirit of learning and cultural appreciation.

Their challenge is remembering that wisdom includes both logic and intuition.

Virgo in the Tenth House

The Dedicated Professional

Virgo in the Tenth House often produces individuals who gain recognition through dedication and reliability.

Their careers may involve service, research, healing professions, education, or technical fields.

They are often respected for their attention to detail and ability to solve problems.

However, they must avoid placing too much pressure on themselves to meet impossible standards.

True mastery grows through patience rather than perfection.

Virgo in the Eleventh House

The Helpful Visionary

With Virgo in the Eleventh House, individuals often contribute practical skills to social groups or humanitarian causes.

They may help organize projects, coordinate events, or support community initiatives.

Friends may rely on them for thoughtful advice and practical solutions.

Their challenge is learning that not every problem needs immediate correction; sometimes, presence and encouragement are enough.

Virgo in the Twelfth House

The Quiet Healer

Virgo in the Twelfth House blends analytical ability with spiritual sensitivity.

These individuals may possess deep intuitive understanding of human suffering and healing.

They may feel drawn toward meditation, spiritual study, counseling, or healing arts that work quietly behind the scenes.

Their challenge is learning to trust their inner wisdom rather than doubting themselves.

Often their greatest strength lies in compassion and silent service.

Reflection

Virgo teaches the sacred art of refinement.

Where Leo encourages us to shine, Virgo reminds us to care for the light we carry.

Through patience, observation, and thoughtful effort, Virgo energy transforms raw potential into meaningful contribution.

Its wisdom reminds us that greatness often grows through small daily acts of dedication.

The Journey Continues

Chapter 32 carries you beyond what has been learned and into what must now be *lived.* After the sweeping perspective of the eternal journey, the next step is not another concept; it is a commitment to embodiment. Wisdom becomes real when it shapes your choices, your tone, your courage, and the way you return to yourself in ordinary moments.

The soul does not evolve in a single breakthrough. It evolves through repetition made sacred, through the quiet decision to begin again with more awareness than before. You will recognize familiar crossroads, familiar emotions, and familiar tests of faith, and you may realize you are meeting them differently now. That is the sign of growth. The spiral is still turning, but you are standing on higher ground.

As the path continues, you are invited to hold both truth and tenderness: to honor who you have been, while making room for who you are becoming. Let what you have learned become a living practice. Let your inner light guide you when the way feels unclear. And remember, no chapter ever truly ends. It simply opens into the next becoming.

CHAPTER 33: LIBRA THROUGH THE HOUSES, THE PATH OF BALANCE

The Spirit of Libra

Libra is the seventh sign of the zodiac and represents balance, harmony, justice, and relationships.

Its symbol is the Scales, reminding us that life constantly seeks equilibrium. Libra teaches that no soul grows entirely alone. We evolve through connection, reflection, and the exchange of energy with others.

Libra is ruled by Venus, the planet of love, beauty, and attraction. Under Venus, Libra seeks elegance in relationships and fairness in human interaction.

Where Virgo seeks improvement through effort, Libra seeks improvement through cooperation and understanding.

Libra energy encourages diplomacy, grace, and the ability to see life from multiple perspectives.

Where Libra appears in the birth chart reveals where the soul seeks partnership, harmony, and aesthetic balance.

Let us explore how Libra expresses itself through the twelve houses.

Libra in the First House

The Diplomatic Presence

When Libra appears in the First House, individuals often possess natural charm and grace.

They may be socially aware and instinctively sensitive to the emotional atmosphere around them.

Their presence often brings calm and balance into group settings.

However, their challenge is learning to maintain their own identity rather than constantly adjusting to please others.

True harmony begins with inner balance.

Libra in the Second House

The Lover of Beauty and Comfort

With Libra in the Second House, individuals often value beauty, art, and harmonious surroundings.

They may spend money on aesthetics, fashion, or artistic objects that bring pleasure to the senses.

Financial success may come through partnerships or creative fields.

Their deeper lesson is learning to develop self-worth that is not dependent upon approval or external validation.

Libra in the Third House

The Thoughtful Communicator

Libra in the Third House creates individuals who are diplomatic and persuasive in their speech.

They often excel in negotiation, teaching, counseling, or writing.

Their ability to see both sides of an issue allows them to communicate ideas with fairness and understanding.

However, indecision may arise when they try too hard to weigh every possible perspective.

Libra in the Fourth House

The Harmonious Home Builder

When Libra appears in the Fourth House, individuals often seek peace and beauty within their home environment.

They may enjoy decorating or creating living spaces that feel balanced and welcoming.

Family relationships often become important areas for learning compromise and emotional diplomacy.

Their challenge is avoiding the suppression of personal feelings in order to maintain peace.

Libra in the Fifth House

The Romantic Artist

With Libra in the Fifth House, creativity often expresses itself through art, music, design, or performance.

Romantic relationships may feel deeply important, and individuals with this placement often enjoy courtship and emotional connection.

They may be naturally charming and attractive to others.

The lesson here is remembering that authentic love thrives through honesty as well as beauty.

Libra in the Sixth House

The Cooperative Worker

When Libra influences the Sixth House, individuals often prefer collaborative work environments.

They may excel in professions involving counseling, law, design, mediation, or diplomacy.

Their sense of fairness often guides how they treat coworkers and clients.

However, they must learn to address conflict directly rather than avoiding difficult conversations.

Libra in the Seventh House

The True Partner

Libra feels especially powerful in the Seventh House, which it naturally governs.

Individuals with this placement often seek meaningful partnerships and may feel incomplete without a significant relationship.

Marriage, business partnerships, or close alliances often become central life themes.

Their growth comes through learning that healthy relationships require equality, honesty, and mutual respect.

Libra in the Eighth House

The Harmonizer of Deep Bonds

Libra in the Eighth House brings diplomacy into areas involving shared resources, emotional transformation, and intimate partnerships.

Individuals with this placement may carefully navigate complex financial or emotional situations involving others.

They often seek balance in relationships that involve power or vulnerability.

Their lesson is learning to trust emotional depth without losing their sense of equilibrium.

Libra in the Ninth House

The Seeker of Universal Justice

When Libra occupies the Ninth House, individuals often pursue philosophy, law, or spiritual teachings centered around fairness and ethics.

They may feel drawn toward exploring cultures, religions, or belief systems that emphasize peace and cooperation.

Travel and education often broaden their understanding of human harmony.

Their challenge is developing firm beliefs rather than endlessly weighing opposing views.

Libra in the Tenth House

The Diplomatic Leader

With Libra in the Tenth House, individuals may build careers in law, public relations, diplomacy, design, or leadership roles requiring negotiation.

They often possess the ability to mediate conflicts and guide others toward fair solutions.

Their public image may reflect grace, refinement, and professionalism.

However, they must ensure that their decisions are guided by integrity rather than popularity.

Libra in the Eleventh House

The Social Visionary

Libra in the Eleventh House brings balance into social groups and collective movements.

These individuals often value cooperation within communities and may enjoy participating in organizations that promote justice or humanitarian causes.

They often form friendships based on shared ideals.

Their lesson is remembering that even within groups, individuality still matters.

Libra in the Twelfth House

The Hidden Peacemaker

When Libra appears in the Twelfth House, individuals often possess deep compassion and a quiet desire to bring peace into the world.

They may work behind the scenes, helping others resolve conflicts or emotional struggles.

Spiritual growth may come through forgiveness, understanding, and the release of resentment.

Their challenge is learning to honor their own needs while offering harmony to others.

Reflection

Libra reminds us that life is not only about personal growth but also about shared experience.

Through relationships, we learn empathy, cooperation, and the delicate balance between individuality and unity.

Libra teaches that beauty, fairness, and peace are not passive qualities; they are conscious choices we make every day.

The Journey Continues

After Libra establishes harmony and balance in relationships, the zodiac moves into a deeper and more mysterious realm.

The next sign invites the soul to explore transformation, power, and emotional depth.

CHAPTER 34:
SCORPIO THROUGH THE HOUSES, THE PATH OF TRANSFORMATION

The Spirit of Scorpio

Scorpio is the eighth sign of the zodiac and represents transformation, intensity, regeneration, and the deep mysteries of life and death.

Its symbol is the Scorpion, a creature that survives in harsh environments and carries powerful defensive instincts. Yet Scorpio's deeper symbol is often the Phoenix, the mythical bird that rises from its own ashes, representing rebirth and spiritual evolution.

Scorpio is ruled traditionally by Mars, the planet of action and courage, and in modern astrology by Pluto, the planet of transformation and hidden power.

Wherever Scorpio appears in a birth chart, we find areas where the soul experiences deep emotional encounters, psychological insight, and profound inner change.

Scorpio energy does not remain on the surface. It seeks truth beneath appearances and invites the soul to face what is hidden, unresolved, or misunderstood.

Through this process, Scorpio reveals one of life's greatest teachings:

What we transform within ourselves becomes the source of our greatest strength.

Let us explore how Scorpio expresses itself through the twelve houses.

Scorpio in the First House

The Magnetic Presence

When Scorpio occupies the First House, individuals often possess an intense and mysterious presence.

Others may feel drawn to them without fully understanding why.

These individuals often carry strong willpower and emotional depth.

They may undergo several major personal transformations throughout life, emerging stronger each time.

Their lesson is learning to trust others rather than always guarding their inner world.

Scorpio in the Second House

The Transformer of Values

With Scorpio in the Second House, individuals often experience profound changes in their attitudes toward money, security, and personal values.

Financial matters may involve cycles of gain and loss that teach deeper lessons about self-worth.

These individuals often develop strong resourcefulness and resilience.

Their ultimate realization is that true security lies not in possessions but in inner strength.

Scorpio in the Third House

The Investigator of Truth

Scorpio in the Third House creates minds that seek hidden knowledge.

These individuals often enjoy research, psychology, investigative work, or studying subjects that reveal deeper truths about human nature.

Their communication style may be powerful and persuasive.

However, they must learn to share knowledge constructively rather than using information as a form of control.

Scorpio in the Fourth House

The Deep Emotional Roots

When Scorpio appears in the Fourth House, individuals often experience powerful emotional ties to family and ancestry.

Early life may involve intense experiences that shape emotional resilience.

These individuals may feel compelled to understand their family history or heal generational patterns.

Their lesson is learning that emotional healing can free the soul from the past.

Scorpio in the Fifth House

The Passionate Creator

Scorpio in the Fifth House brings emotional depth into creativity, romance, and personal expression.

These individuals may experience intense romantic relationships and powerful artistic inspiration.

Creative projects may reflect themes of transformation, mystery, or emotional exploration.

Their challenge is learning to balance passion with emotional stability.

Scorpio in the Sixth House

The Healer of Hidden Wounds

With Scorpio in the Sixth House, individuals may feel drawn toward professions involving healing, psychology, medicine, or crisis support.

They often possess strong intuition regarding the emotional or physical needs of others.

Their work may involve helping people through periods of transformation or recovery.

The lesson here is remembering to care for their own well-being while helping others.

Scorpio in the Seventh House

The Transformational Partner

When Scorpio influences the Seventh House, relationships often become powerful catalysts for personal growth.

Partnerships may be intense and emotionally transformative.

These individuals often seek deep connection rather than superficial companionship.

However, they must guard against jealousy, possessiveness, or power struggles within relationships.

True intimacy grows through trust and emotional honesty.

Scorpio in the Eighth House

The Master of Transformation

Scorpio feels especially powerful in the Eighth House, which it naturally governs.

Individuals with this placement often possess profound insight into the mysteries of life, death, psychology, and spiritual transformation.

They may feel drawn toward healing arts, spiritual research, or uncovering hidden truths.

Their journey often involves learning how to guide themselves and others through periods of emotional rebirth.

Scorpio in the Ninth House

The Seeker of Hidden Wisdom

When Scorpio appears in the Ninth House, individuals often explore philosophy, religion, or spiritual traditions that reveal deeper layers of existence.

They may be fascinated by ancient knowledge, mystical teachings, or psychological insight.

Travel and study often become journeys of personal transformation.

Their challenge is avoiding rigid belief systems and remaining open to evolving wisdom.

Scorpio in the Tenth House

The Powerful Achiever

Scorpios in the Tenth House often produce individuals who pursue careers involving leadership, research, psychology, healing, or transformative social work.

They may rise to positions of authority through determination and strategic insight.

However, they must ensure their ambition serves a meaningful purpose rather than personal power alone.

When aligned with integrity, they become agents of powerful change.

Scorpio in the Eleventh House

The Intense Visionary

With Scorpio in the Eleventh House, individuals often bring emotional depth into friendships and social causes.

They may be drawn to groups dedicated to transformation, healing, or uncovering hidden truths.

Their friendships may be few but deeply meaningful.

Their challenge is learning to trust collective efforts without feeling the need to control outcomes.

Scorpio in the Twelfth House

The Mystic of the Hidden Realm

Scorpio in the Twelfth House connects transformation with spirituality and the subconscious mind.

These individuals often possess strong intuitive or psychic awareness.

They may feel drawn toward meditation, spiritual healing, dream work, or exploring the unseen dimensions of existence.

Their challenge is releasing fear of the unknown and embracing the profound wisdom that emerges from inner exploration.

Reflection

Scorpio teaches the soul one of life's deepest truths:

Transformation is not something to fear; it is the path of renewal.

Through endings, revelations, and emotional courage, Scorpio energy allows the soul to shed old identities and rise into new awareness.

It reminds us that every experience, even those that appear painful, contains the seeds of profound personal power.

The Journey Continues

Chapter 34 arrives as a quiet but powerful threshold, one where insight asks to become *practice*, and practice asks to become *identity*. What you have learned so far is no longer meant to stay in the mind alone. It is meant to shape the way you choose, the way you love, and the way you return to yourself when life feels uncertain.

At this stage of the journey, growth often looks less like dramatic change and more like steady devotion. You may find yourself meeting familiar patterns again, but with a new kind of strength, pausing sooner, listening deeper, responding with more integrity. This is the soul's refinement: the same lessons, met with a wiser heart.

The path ahead will continue to unfold in seasons, some expansive, some inward, some challenging, some blessed. Let Chapter 34 remind you that you do not have to rush the becoming. You only have to stay present to it. Trust what is unfolding, honor what is being asked of you, and keep walking, one conscious step at a time.

CHAPTER 35: SAGITTARIUS THROUGH THE HOUSES, THE PATH OF EXPANSION

The Spirit of Sagittarius

Sagittarius is the ninth sign of the zodiac and represents expansion, exploration, wisdom, and the search for truth.

Its symbol is the Archer, a centaur aiming an arrow toward the sky. This image reflects the Sagittarius desire to reach beyond ordinary limitations and discover higher understanding.

Sagittarius is ruled by Jupiter, the largest planet in our solar system and the traditional ruler of growth, opportunity, philosophy, and spiritual insight.

Where Scorpio explored the depths of life, Sagittarius now lifts the soul toward the horizon of possibility.

Sagittarius teaches us that life is a journey of discovery. It encourages curiosity, faith, and the willingness to explore both the world and the mind.

Where Sagittarius appears in a birth chart reveals where the soul longs to grow, learn, and experience the vastness of existence.

Let us explore how Sagittarius expresses its adventurous spirit through the twelve houses.

Sagittarius in the First House

The Explorer of Life

When Sagittarius appears in the First House, individuals often possess an open, enthusiastic personality.

They may appear optimistic, adventurous, and eager to explore new experiences.

Others often perceive them as friendly and inspiring.

Their life journey often involves travel, learning, and personal discovery.

Their challenge is learning to balance enthusiasm with focus and follow-through.

Sagittarius in the Second House

The Seeker of Abundance

With Sagittarius in the Second House, individuals often view money and resources as tools for freedom and exploration.

They may enjoy spending on travel, education, or meaningful experiences.

Financial opportunities may arise through teaching, publishing, international ventures, or philosophy-related fields.

Their lesson is learning to balance generosity with responsible planning.

Sagittarius in the Third House

The Storyteller

Sagittarius in the Third House brings enthusiasm into communication.

These individuals often enjoy sharing ideas, telling stories, and discussing philosophy or global issues.

Their curiosity may lead them to explore many different subjects.

They may become teachers, writers, or public speakers.

However, they must learn to balance big ideas with attention to detail.

Sagittarius in the Fourth House

The Seeker of a Meaningful Home

When Sagittarius occupies the Fourth House, individuals often seek a home environment that feels expansive and inspiring.

They may enjoy living in different places throughout life or creating homes filled with books, cultural influences, and learning.

Family traditions may emphasize freedom and personal growth.

Their challenge is learning that emotional grounding is just as important as exploration.

Sagittarius in the Fifth House

The Joyful Creator

With Sagittarius in the Fifth House, creativity often expresses itself through adventure, performance, and bold ideas.

These individuals may enjoy sports, travel, artistic exploration, or teaching through entertainment.

Romantic relationships may be exciting and filled with shared experiences.

Their lesson is balancing freedom with emotional commitment.

Sagittarius in the Sixth House

The Purposeful Worker

When Sagittarius influences the Sixth House, individuals often seek work that feels meaningful and aligned with personal values.

They may enjoy careers involving education, travel, philosophy, or helping others expand their perspectives.

Routine tasks may feel restrictive unless they contribute to a larger purpose.

Their challenge is learning discipline while maintaining inspiration.

Sagittarius in the Seventh House

The Adventurous Partner

Sagittarius in the Seventh House often brings relationships that involve travel, learning, or cultural exchange.

Partners may share a love for exploration or intellectual growth.

These individuals often value honesty and independence within relationships.

However, they must learn to balance personal freedom with commitment.

Sagittarius in the Eighth House

The Spiritual Investigator

With Sagittarius in the Eighth House, individuals often explore the deeper mysteries of life through philosophy, spirituality, or psychology.

They may study metaphysical traditions or seek meaning in life's transformative experiences.

Financial partnerships may involve shared investments or opportunities related to global ventures.

Their lesson is learning that true wisdom includes emotional understanding as well as intellectual insight.

Sagittarius in the Ninth House

The Philosopher

Sagittarius feels completely at home in the Ninth House, which it naturally governs.

Individuals with this placement often feel drawn toward higher education, philosophy, religion, or international travel.

They may become teachers, spiritual guides, writers, or explorers of cultural wisdom.

Their challenge is remembering that learning is an ongoing journey rather than a final destination.

Sagittarius in the Tenth House

The Visionary Leader

Sagittarius in the Tenth House often leads individuals toward careers involving education, law, publishing, travel, or spiritual leadership.

They may inspire others through their wisdom, optimism, and broad perspective.

Their ambitions often extend beyond personal success toward contributing to the greater good.

Their lesson is learning patience and persistence when pursuing long-term goals.

Sagittarius in the Eleventh House

The Global Humanitarian

With Sagittarius in the Eleventh House, individuals often feel inspired to contribute to causes that benefit humanity.

They may become involved in international organizations, educational initiatives, or social movements promoting freedom and understanding.

Friendships may span many cultures and backgrounds.

Their challenge is learning to turn visionary ideas into practical action.

Sagittarius in the Twelfth House

The Mystic Explorer

Sagittarius in the Twelfth House brings spiritual exploration into the inner world.

These individuals may seek meaning through meditation, philosophy, spiritual study, or quiet contemplation.

They may feel guided by a strong sense of faith or divine purpose.

Their greatest strength lies in their ability to trust the unseen wisdom that guides their path.

Reflection

Sagittarius reminds us that life is an endless journey of discovery.

It teaches the soul to seek truth beyond limitation, to explore new horizons, and to embrace the wisdom found through experience.

Through its expansive spirit, Sagittarius encourages us to remain curious, hopeful, and open to the many possibilities life offers.

The Journey Continues

After Sagittarius expands the mind and spirit, the zodiac moves into a sign that brings structure and mastery.

The next step in the soul's evolution involves discipline, responsibility, and the building of lasting achievements.

CHAPTER 36:
CAPRICORN THROUGH THE HOUSES, THE PATH OF MASTERY

The Spirit of Capricorn

Capricorn is the tenth sign of the zodiac and represents discipline, endurance, responsibility, and long-term achievement.

Its symbol is the Sea-Goat, a mythical creature with the body of a goat and the tail of a fish. This unusual symbol represents Capricorn's unique ability to move between two worlds, the emotional depths of life and the towering heights of ambition.

Capricorn is ruled by Saturn, the planet associated with time, structure, wisdom, and karmic lessons. Saturn teaches that true achievement is not gained quickly. Instead, it develops through patience, persistence, and experience.

Capricorn energy reminds us that life is not only about dreams and inspiration, it is also about building something meaningful that endures through time.

Where Capricorn appears in the birth chart reveals where the soul is learning maturity, responsibility, and mastery through effort.

Let us explore how Capricorn expresses its determined strength through the twelve houses.

Capricorn in the First House

The Determined Individual

When Capricorn appears in the First House, individuals often present themselves with seriousness, dignity, and quiet strength.

They may appear reserved in early life, but beneath this calm exterior lies powerful determination.

These individuals often mature quickly and may take on responsibility earlier than others.

Their life journey often involves learning confidence and allowing themselves moments of joy rather than constant duty.

Capricorn in the Second House

The Builder of Security

With Capricorn in the Second House, individuals often approach finances and material resources with caution and discipline.

They may work patiently to build financial stability over time.

Rather than seeking quick success, they often focus on long-term security and responsible management.

Their lesson is learning that true worth includes emotional and spiritual richness as well as material stability.

Capricorn in the Third House

The Serious Thinker

Capricorn in the Third House produces individuals with practical and disciplined minds.

Their communication style may be thoughtful and deliberate.

They often excel in fields that require careful planning, strategy, or structured thinking.

However, they must remember that curiosity and creativity are just as important as discipline.

Capricorn in the Fourth House

The Guardian of Legacy

When Capricorn occupies the Fourth House, individuals often feel a strong sense of responsibility toward family and heritage.

They may seek to build a stable home environment and establish traditions that endure.

Their early life may involve experiences that teach resilience.

Their lesson is learning to nurture emotional warmth alongside responsibility.

Capricorn in the Fifth House

The Disciplined Creator

With Capricorn in the Fifth House, creativity often develops through persistence and refinement.

These individuals may excel in artistic or intellectual pursuits that require long-term dedication.

Romantic relationships may be approached with seriousness and loyalty.

Their challenge is allowing themselves to experience joy and spontaneity without feeling the need to control every outcome.

Capricorn in the Sixth House

The Dedicated Worker

Capricorn in the Sixth House often produces individuals who take their responsibilities very seriously.

They may excel in careers requiring discipline, organization, and endurance.

Their work ethic may inspire respect from colleagues.

However, they must guard against becoming overwhelmed by duty or neglecting their own well-being.

Balance between effort and rest becomes essential.

Capricorn in the Seventh House

The Responsible Partner

When Capricorn influences the Seventh House, relationships may be approached with seriousness and commitment.

Individuals with this placement often value loyalty, stability, and long-term partnership.

They may be drawn toward mature or ambitious partners.

However, they must remember that emotional warmth is just as important as reliability in relationships.

Capricorn in the Eighth House

The Strategic Transformer

With Capricorn in the Eighth House, individuals often approach deep emotional or financial matters with caution and strategic thinking.

They may possess strong abilities in managing shared resources or navigating complex financial situations.

Their life may involve gradual transformation through responsibility and maturity.

Their lesson is learning to trust emotional vulnerability rather than maintaining constant control.

Capricorn in the Ninth House

The Wise Scholar

Capricorn in the Ninth House brings discipline into philosophy, education, and spiritual study.

Individuals may pursue higher knowledge with serious dedication.

They often seek practical wisdom that can be applied in real-world situations.

Travel and education may become tools for building meaningful achievements.

Their challenge is remaining open to inspiration and new perspectives.

Capricorn in the Tenth House

The Master Builder

Capricorn feels especially powerful in the Tenth House, which it naturally governs.

Individuals with this placement often feel a strong drive to achieve recognition and build lasting accomplishments.

Their careers may involve leadership, government, business, engineering, or fields requiring strategic planning.

Their life journey often involves climbing steadily toward success.

However, they must remember that true leadership includes compassion as well as authority.

Capricorn in the Eleventh House

The Organizer of Vision

With Capricorn in the Eleventh House, individuals often bring structure and discipline into group efforts and social causes.

They may take leadership roles within organizations or community initiatives.

Their long-term planning abilities allow them to turn ideas into practical results.

Their lesson is remembering that collaboration and friendship are as important as accomplishment.

Capricorn in the Twelfth House

The Silent Endurer

Capricorn in the Twelfth House connects discipline with the inner spiritual world.

These individuals may quietly carry heavy responsibilities or emotional burdens.

They often possess deep inner strength and resilience.

Spiritual growth may come through reflection, solitude, and learning to release unnecessary burdens.

Their challenge is discovering that vulnerability can also be a source of strength.

Reflection

Capricorn teaches the soul the value of patience, endurance, and responsibility.

While other signs may focus on inspiration or emotional exploration, Capricorn reminds us that dreams become reality only when supported by dedication and perseverance.

Through Capricorn's wisdom, the soul learns that true success is not measured only by achievement but by the character developed along the journey.

The Journey Continues

After Capricorn builds structure and mastery, the zodiac moves into a sign that brings innovation and vision for the future.

CHAPTER 37: AQUARIUS THROUGH THE HOUSES, THE PATH OF AWAKENING

The Spirit of Aquarius

Aquarius is the eleventh sign of the zodiac and represents innovation, humanitarian ideals, freedom, and the evolution of human consciousness.

Its symbol is the Water Bearer, a figure pouring streams of knowledge and insight upon the world. Unlike the emotional waters of Cancer or Pisces, Aquarius pours the waters of awareness, ideas that awaken humanity to new possibilities.

Aquarius is ruled traditionally by Saturn, the planet of structure and wisdom, and in modern astrology by Uranus, the planet of invention, sudden insight, and revolutionary change.

This combination creates a fascinating paradox: Aquarius seeks both stability and transformation. It honors wisdom from the past while also daring to imagine a future that has never existed before.

Where Aquarius appears in a birth chart, we find areas where the soul is called to think differently, challenge limitations, and contribute to collective progress.

Aquarius reminds us that every generation carries the responsibility of helping humanity evolve.

Let us explore how Aquarius expresses its awakening energy through the twelve houses.

Aquarius in the First House

The Unique Individual

When Aquarius appears in the First House, individuals often possess a distinctive personality and original outlook on life.

They may seem unconventional or ahead of their time.

Others often notice their independence and strong desire to follow their own path.

These individuals are often innovators who inspire others to think differently.

Their lesson is learning to balance individuality with emotional connection.

Aquarius in the Second House

The Innovator of Resources

With Aquarius in the Second House, individuals may approach finances and values in unusual or progressive ways.

They may earn money through technology, innovation, humanitarian work, or unconventional ventures.

Material possessions may be less important than freedom and intellectual exploration.

Their challenge is learning practical stability while maintaining visionary thinking.

Aquarius in the Third House

The Visionary Thinker

Aquarius in the Third House produces minds that thrive on new ideas.

These individuals often enjoy science, philosophy, technology, or social reform.

Their communication style may be inventive and intellectually stimulating.

They often bring fresh perspectives into discussions.

However, they must remember that emotional sensitivity is just as important as intellectual brilliance.

Aquarius in the Fourth House

The Unconventional Home

When Aquarius occupies the Fourth House, individuals may experience unique or unconventional family environments.

Their homes may become places of creativity, innovation, or community gatherings.

They may feel a strong desire to create a living space that reflects freedom and originality.

Their lesson is learning to balance independence with emotional belonging.

Aquarius in the Fifth House

The Creative Visionary

With Aquarius in the Fifth House, creativity often expresses itself through originality and experimentation.

These individuals may enjoy inventing new forms of art, technology, or performance.

Romantic relationships may feel exciting and unconventional.

Their challenge is learning to remain emotionally present rather than maintaining emotional distance.

Aquarius in the Sixth House

The Progressive Worker

Aquarius in the Sixth House brings innovation into work and daily routines.

Individuals with this placement may seek careers involving technology, research, social reform, or humanitarian efforts.

They often prefer work environments that encourage independence and creative thinking.

Their lesson is balancing freedom with practical responsibility.

Aquarius in the Seventh House

The Unconventional Partner

When Aquarius influences the Seventh House, relationships often involve strong intellectual connections and mutual respect for independence.

Partners may share progressive ideas or unconventional lifestyles.

Friendship may become the foundation of romantic relationships.

However, emotional closeness must be cultivated alongside intellectual compatibility.

Aquarius in the Eighth House

The Explorer of Hidden Forces

Aquarius in the Eighth House often brings curiosity about the unseen forces of life.

Individuals may explore psychology, metaphysics, science, or transformational healing methods.

They may feel fascinated by mysteries that combine science and spirituality.

Their lesson is learning to balance intellectual understanding with emotional depth.

Aquarius in the Ninth House

The Revolutionary Philosopher

With Aquarius in the Ninth House, individuals often seek new ways of understanding philosophy, spirituality, and human potential.

They may challenge traditional belief systems and explore innovative ideas about society and consciousness.

Travel and education often expand their awareness of humanity's shared future.

Their challenge is remaining open to wisdom from both tradition and innovation.

Aquarius in the Tenth House

The Visionary Leader

Aquarius in the Tenth House often produces leaders who introduce progressive ideas into society.

Their careers may involve science, technology, humanitarian work, social reform, or visionary leadership.

They often strive to make a lasting contribution that benefits humanity as a whole.

Their lesson is learning patience when introducing new ideas that others may not immediately understand.

Aquarius in the Eleventh House

The Humanitarian Visionary

Aquarius feels especially powerful in the Eleventh House, which it naturally governs.

Individuals with this placement often feel deeply connected to humanity and may dedicate themselves to causes that promote equality and progress.

Friendships and group efforts often become sources of inspiration.

They may help create communities that encourage freedom, creativity, and shared vision.

Aquarius in the Twelfth House

The Cosmic Dreamer

Aquarius in the Twelfth House blends visionary thinking with spiritual awareness.

These individuals may feel connected to collective consciousness or future possibilities.

They may experience powerful dreams, intuitive insights, or inspiration that seems to come from beyond ordinary awareness.

Their challenge is grounding their visions in practical action so that their ideas can benefit others.

Reflection

Aquarius reminds us that humanity is always evolving.

It encourages the soul to step beyond old limitations and imagine a future filled with greater understanding, cooperation, and innovation.

Aquarius teaches that each individual carries a spark of originality that can help illuminate the path forward.

Through courage, creativity, and compassion, we become part of humanity's unfolding story.

The Journey Continues

After Aquarius awakens the mind to the future, the zodiac moves into the final sign of the cycle.

The last stage of the journey invites the soul to return to compassion, intuition, and spiritual unity.

CHAPTER 38:
PISCES THROUGH THE HOUSES, THE PATH OF COMPASSION

The Spirit of Pisces

Pisces is the twelfth and final sign of the zodiac, representing compassion, intuition, imagination, and spiritual unity.

Its symbol is two fish swimming in opposite directions, reflecting the dual nature of Pisces. One fish moves toward the material world while the other swims toward spiritual transcendence. This symbol reminds us that the soul is constantly navigating between earthly experience and divine awareness.

Pisces is ruled traditionally by Jupiter, the planet of wisdom and spiritual expansion, and in modern astrology by Neptune, the planet associated with dreams, intuition, imagination, and mystical awareness.

Where Aquarius awakens the mind, Pisces opens the heart and soul.

Pisces energy dissolves boundaries. It reminds us that behind our individual identities lies a deeper truth: all life is connected.

Where Pisces appears in the birth chart reveals where the soul seeks compassion, healing, creativity, and spiritual understanding.

Let us explore how Pisces expresses its gentle and profound influence through the twelve houses.

Pisces in the First House

The Sensitive Presence

When Pisces appears in the First House, individuals often possess a gentle, compassionate nature.

Others may sense their emotional sensitivity and kindness.

They often carry a deep imagination and may feel strongly connected to music, art, or spiritual awareness.

However, they must learn to maintain healthy boundaries so that they do not absorb the emotions of others too deeply.

Pisces in the Second House

The Spiritual Relationship with Value

With Pisces in the Second House, individuals often view money and possessions through an emotional or spiritual lens.

They may feel generous and willing to share resources with others.

Creative talents such as music, art, or healing work may become sources of income.

Their lesson is learning to balance compassion with practical financial awareness.

Pisces in the Third House

The Intuitive Communicator

Pisces in the Third House brings imagination and empathy into communication.

These individuals may express themselves through poetry, storytelling, music, or visual art.

Their minds often move fluidly between logic and intuition.

However, they must learn to organize their thoughts clearly so that their ideas can be understood by others.

Pisces in the Fourth House

The Dreamer of Home

When Pisces occupies the Fourth House, individuals often seek emotional peace and spiritual comfort within their home environment.

They may feel deeply connected to family memories and ancestral influences.

Their homes may become places of creativity, healing, or quiet reflection.

Their challenge is learning to ground emotional sensitivity in practical stability.

Pisces in the Fifth House

The Inspired Creator

With Pisces in the Fifth House, creativity often flows naturally through imagination and emotion.

These individuals may feel drawn to music, painting, writing, or other artistic forms that express deep feeling.

Romantic relationships may feel magical or idealized.

Their lesson is learning to balance dreams with realistic expectations.

Pisces in the Sixth House

The Compassionate Helper

Pisces in the Sixth House often produces individuals who feel called to help others.

They may work in healing professions, counseling, spiritual guidance, or charitable service.

Their empathy allows them to sense the emotional needs of those around them.

However, they must remember to care for their own health and emotional well-being.

Pisces in the Seventh House

The Romantic Idealist

When Pisces influences the Seventh House, relationships often feel deeply emotional and spiritually meaningful.

Individuals with this placement may seek partners who share compassion and understanding.

They may idealize relationships and hope for deep soul connections.

Their lesson is learning to see partners clearly while still honoring love and empathy.

Pisces in the Eighth House

The Mystic Transformer

Pisces in the Eighth House brings spiritual awareness into the realms of transformation and emotional depth.

These individuals may explore mystical traditions, psychic awareness, or spiritual healing.

They may experience powerful intuitive insights about life's deeper mysteries.

Their challenge is maintaining clarity when exploring emotional or spiritual depths.

Pisces in the Ninth House

The Spiritual Seeker

With Pisces in the Ninth House, individuals often pursue spiritual philosophy and universal compassion.

They may feel drawn toward meditation, mystical teachings, or global humanitarian ideals.

Travel and education may deepen their understanding of humanity's shared spiritual journey.

Their lesson is grounding spiritual beliefs in practical wisdom.

Pisces in the Tenth House

The Compassionate Leader

Pisces in the Tenth House often produces individuals whose careers involve healing, creativity, spirituality, or helping others.

They may become artists, counselors, spiritual guides, or compassionate leaders.

Their public image may reflect kindness and empathy.

However, they must learn to maintain clear boundaries within professional responsibilities.

Pisces in the Eleventh House

The Dreamer of Unity

With Pisces in the Eleventh House, individuals often feel inspired by visions of unity and peace within humanity.

They may participate in humanitarian efforts, artistic communities, or spiritual groups.

Friendships may feel deeply meaningful and emotionally supportive.

Their lesson is balancing idealistic visions with practical action.

Pisces in the Twelfth House

The Soul of the Zodiac

Pisces feels deeply at home in the Twelfth House, which it naturally governs.

Individuals with this placement often possess profound spiritual sensitivity.

They may experience vivid dreams, strong intuition, or a natural connection with the unseen realms of consciousness.

Their lives may involve deep inner reflection, meditation, or spiritual exploration.

Their challenge is remaining grounded while embracing their spiritual gifts.

Reflection

Pisces completes the great journey of the zodiac.

Where Aries began the cycle with the spark of individuality, Pisces dissolves that identity into the awareness that all life is interconnected.

Pisces teaches compassion, forgiveness, imagination, and spiritual unity.

Through its gentle wisdom, we learn that every experience, joyful or painful, has contributed to the soul's growth.

The zodiac journey reminds us that life is not simply a sequence of events but a sacred cycle of evolution.

The Journey Continues

Although Pisces concludes the zodiac cycle, it also prepares the soul for new beginnings.

Every ending contains the seed of another beginning.

Just as the zodiac returns to Aries, life itself continually renews and evolves.

PART IV:

THE SOUL THROUGH THE HOUSES

CHAPTER 39:
THE SOUL IN THE FIRST HOUSE

Awakening to Identity

The First House represents the moment the soul arrives on Earth.

It is the gateway of incarnation, the point where spirit meets form.

In this house, the soul begins to experience individuality. For the first time, it senses the boundary between "self" and "other."

This is the house of identity, presence, and physical life.

The First House is associated with the Ascendant, the sign rising on the eastern horizon at the moment of birth. It describes the way the soul first presents itself to the world.

Here, the soul asks a fundamental question:

Who am I in this life?

The First Breath

The First House is symbolically connected to the moment a newborn takes its first breath.

With that breath, spirit enters the body and consciousness awakens within physical reality.

Everything in the First House reflects the soul's first impressions of the world:

- The body
- The personality
- The instinctive responses to life

It represents how the soul steps forward into existence.

The Birth of Individuality

Before entering this life, the soul existed within a broader spiritual awareness.

But incarnation requires something new, the experience of individuality.

The First House teaches the soul to say:

"I am."

This realization is essential for growth.

Without individuality, the soul could not make choices, develop strengths, or explore unique experiences.

Yet the First House also contains an important lesson.

While the soul learns to express individuality, it must also remember that identity is only one layer of existence.

Behind personality lies the deeper essence of the soul itself.

Instinct and Courage

The First House is associated with instinctive action.

It governs the way we respond immediately to new experiences.

Some souls enter life boldly, eager to explore. Others approach cautiously, observing before acting.

Both approaches are valid expressions of the soul's unfolding journey.

Through the First House the soul learns courage, the willingness to step into the unknown and participate fully in life.

The Mask and the Essence

Astrologers sometimes describe the First House as the "mask" we wear in the world.

But this mask is not deception.

It is the tool the soul uses to interact with reality.

Just as an actor wears different costumes for different roles, the soul adopts a personality suited to the experiences it wishes to explore.

Yet beneath the personality lies something constant:

The deeper self that observes, learns, and evolves.

The Soul's Lesson Here

The First House teaches the soul several important truths:

- Life begins with self-awareness
- Individuality is necessary for growth
- Courage is required to explore existence
- Identity is only the beginning of the spiritual journey

Once the soul has established a sense of self, it naturally begins asking another question.

If I exist as an individual…

What belongs to me?

This question leads the soul into the next stage of experience.

CHAPTER 40:
THE SOUL IN THE SECOND HOUSE

Discovering Worth

The Second House represents the soul's first encounter with the material world.

Here the soul begins to understand ownership, resources, and personal value. While the First House establishes identity, the Second House teaches the soul how to sustain that identity within the physical world.

This house governs:

- Money and material resources
- Personal possessions
- Physical survival
- Self-worth and inner value

At first glance, the Second House may appear to concern only material matters. But its deeper meaning is far more profound.

The Second House ultimately asks the soul:

What do I truly value?

The First Experiences of Security

In early life, the lessons of the Second House often appear through experiences involving security and stability.

A child learns that food, shelter, clothing, and care are necessary for survival. Through these experiences, the soul begins to understand that life requires resources.

But beyond survival, the Second House also teaches emotional security.

The soul begins to ask:

- Am I safe?
- Am I cared for?
- Do I have what I need to live and grow?

These questions shape the foundation of personal confidence.

Possessions as Symbols

Throughout life, the Second House reveals our relationship with possessions.

But possessions are not important only because they have practical value. They also carry symbolic meaning.

- A treasured object may represent comfort.
- A home may represent safety.
- A career may represent accomplishment.

These material forms become reflections of how the soul perceives its place in the world.

However, the soul eventually learns that possessions are temporary tools, not permanent sources of identity.

The Deeper Meaning of Self-Worth

The most important lesson of the Second House concerns self-worth.

Many people initially measure value through external factors:

Money
Success
Status
Possessions

Yet over time the soul discovers a deeper truth.

True worth does not come from what we own, it comes from who we are.

The soul begins to recognize that character, kindness, wisdom, and creativity possess greater value than any physical object.

When this realization occurs, the Second House transforms from a place of attachment into a place of inner stability.

Learning Stewardship

The Second House also teaches responsibility.

Resources must be managed wisely.

Money must be earned, saved, or shared thoughtfully. Possessions must be cared for. Opportunities must be respected.

Through these experiences, the soul learns stewardship, the ability to handle material life with balance and wisdom.

Some souls experience abundance. Others experience scarcity.

Yet both experiences carry important lessons.

Abundance teaches generosity.

Scarcity teaches resourcefulness and appreciation.

The Soul's Relationship with the Earth

Because the Second House governs material life, it also connects the soul to the Earth itself.

This house reminds us that we live within a physical world filled with natural resources and beauty.

Food grows from the soil.
Water flows through rivers and oceans.
Minerals form deep within the planet.

In this sense, the Second House also reflects humanity's responsibility to care for the Earth.

When the soul respects the resources of the planet, it honors the very foundation that sustains life.

The Soul's Lesson Here

The Second House teaches the soul several essential truths:

- Security is necessary for growth
- Possessions are tools, not identity
- True value lies within the self
- Resources should be handled with wisdom and gratitude

Through these lessons, the soul learns that material life can support spiritual growth when approached with balance.

The Next Step in the Journey

After discovering value and stability, the soul begins to expand its awareness once again.

It starts to explore communication, curiosity, and the exchange of ideas.

The next chapter reveals the stage where the soul begins learning about thought, language, and understanding.

CHAPTER 41:
THE SOUL IN THE THIRD HOUSE

Awakening the Mind

The Third House represents the stage where the soul begins to observe, question, and communicate with the world around it.

If the First House says, *"I am,"* and the Second House asks, *"What do I value?"* then the Third House asks a new and powerful question:

"What can I learn?"

This house governs the development of the mind and our earliest interactions with knowledge. It is associated with:

- Thinking and reasoning
- Language and communication
- Curiosity and exploration
- Early education
- Siblings and close companions
- The exchange of ideas

Here, the soul begins to understand that knowledge itself is a form of connection.

The Awakening of Curiosity

The Third House reflects the moment when the soul becomes fascinated by the world.

A child begins asking endless questions:

Why is the sky blue?
Where do birds go in the winter?
How does the wind move the trees?

These questions are more than childish curiosity. They represent the soul's first attempts to understand the patterns of life.

Through observation and inquiry, the soul begins building a framework of knowledge.

This is the stage where the mind becomes a bridge between inner awareness and the outer world.

The Power of Words

Language becomes one of the most powerful tools of the Third House.

Through words, the soul discovers the ability to:

- Share ideas
- Express feelings
- Ask questions
- Build relationships

Words can inspire hope, create understanding, and spark new possibilities.

Yet words can also wound or mislead if used carelessly.

Thus, the Third House teaches the soul the responsibility that comes with communication.

Learning to speak truthfully and listen thoughtfully becomes a profound part of spiritual growth.

The Role of Learning

Education belongs to the realm of the Third House.

This house governs the early stages of learning, reading, writing, conversation, and basic understanding of the world.

Through these experiences, the soul develops intellectual skills that will serve it throughout life.

But the Third House is not limited to formal schooling.

Learning also happens through daily life:

- Conversations with friends
- Observing nature
- Listening to stories
- Traveling short distances and discovering new places

Every experience becomes a lesson for the growing mind.

Siblings and Early Companions

The Third House also reflects relationships with siblings, cousins, neighbors, and early companions.

These relationships are important because they teach the soul about interaction and cooperation.

Through siblings, the soul learns:

- Sharing
- Competition
- Communication
- Understanding different perspectives

These early relationships often shape how the soul approaches communication throughout life.

The Development of Perspective

One of the most important lessons of the Third House is learning that every person sees the world differently.

Through conversation and experience, the soul begins to realize that other minds exist with their own thoughts, ideas, and interpretations.

This awareness expands understanding.

It teaches humility.

It encourages the soul to remain curious rather than assuming it already knows everything.

The Balance of Knowledge and Wisdom

The Third House gathers information.

But gathering information alone does not create wisdom.

At times, the soul may become overwhelmed by facts, opinions, and endless streams of information.

Eventually, the soul must learn to discern what knowledge is meaningful and what knowledge is merely noise.

This balance between knowledge and understanding prepares the soul for deeper philosophical exploration later in life.

The Soul's Lesson Here

The Third House teaches several important truths:

- Curiosity is the beginning of wisdom
- Words have the power to create connection or division
- Knowledge grows through observation and experience
- Understanding others expands the mind and heart

Through these lessons, the soul begins to realize that learning is a lifelong journey.

The Next Step in the Journey

As the soul develops its mind and communication skills, it begins to seek something deeper than knowledge alone.

After exploring the outer world through curiosity, the soul turns inward toward the foundations of emotional security.

CHAPTER 42:
THE SOUL IN THE FOURTH HOUSE

Returning to the Roots

The Fourth House represents the soul's search for home, emotional security, and the foundation of identity.

If the First House introduced individuality, and the Third House explored the mind, the Fourth House moves inward into the realm of the heart.

Here, the soul begins to ask:

Where do I belong?

This house governs:

- Home and family
- Emotional security
- Ancestry and heritage
- Childhood experiences
- The inner world of feelings
- The spiritual roots of the soul

The Fourth House is often described as the foundation of the birth chart, because it reveals the emotional ground upon which the entire life journey is built.

The Meaning of Home

At first, the soul understands home as a physical place.

It may be a house, an apartment, or a room filled with familiar objects.

But as life unfolds, the soul gradually realizes that home is not merely a structure made of walls and a roof.

True home is an emotional state of safety and acceptance.

It is the place where the soul feels free to rest, heal, and simply exist without pretense.

Some people experience a strong sense of belonging early in life. Others must search for it through many experiences.

Yet the quest for home remains one of the deepest motivations of the human spirit.

The Influence of Family

The Fourth House reflects the family environment into which the soul is born.

Family members often become the first mirrors through which the soul learns about love, trust, and emotional connection.

Parents, grandparents, and ancestors contribute not only genetics but also patterns of belief, behavior, and emotional response.

Some of these patterns nurture growth.

Others present challenges that require healing and transformation.

Through these experiences, the soul begins to understand that it is part of a much larger story, one that stretches across generations.

Ancestral Memory

Many spiritual traditions suggest that the soul carries echoes of ancestral experience.

These echoes may appear as talents, instincts, fears, or emotional tendencies that seem to exist even before personal experience has shaped them.

The Fourth House often reveals these inherited influences.

By understanding family history, the soul can gain insight into patterns that have been passed down through generations.

When the soul becomes aware of these patterns, it gains the ability to transform them, bringing healing not only to itself but to the lineage that came before.

The Inner Sanctuary

As life progresses, the Fourth House begins to represent something even deeper than family or ancestry.

It becomes the inner sanctuary of the soul.

This is the quiet space within where the soul retreats for reflection and renewal.

In this sanctuary the soul can:

- Remember its deeper purpose
- Release emotional burdens
- Reconnect with inner peace

The stronger this inner foundation becomes, the more confidently the soul can move through the outer world.

Healing the Emotional Roots

Not every soul begins life with a strong emotional foundation.

Some encounter instability, loss, or emotional confusion during early years.

Yet even these experiences contain opportunities for growth.

The Fourth House teaches that healing the past is possible.

By acknowledging pain rather than denying it, the soul gradually transforms wounded memories into wisdom.

Over time, the soul learns that home is something it can create within itself.

The Soul's Lesson Here

The Fourth House teaches the soul several profound truths:

- Emotional security is the foundation of growth
- Family influences shape early identity
- Ancestral patterns can be transformed through awareness
- True home ultimately exists within the heart

Through these lessons, the soul learns to nurture itself and others with compassion.

The Turning Point of the Journey

The Fourth House represents the deepest inward point of the chart.

It is the midnight of the soul's daily cycle.

After reaching this point of emotional reflection, the journey begins to move outward again.

From the quiet sanctuary of the Fourth House, the soul begins to rediscover joy, creativity, and the desire to express itself.

CHAPTER 43:
THE SOUL IN THE FIFTH HOUSE

The Birth of Creativity

The Fifth House is the house of joy, creativity, love, and personal expression.

After the soul has developed its identity, values, thoughts, and emotional foundation, it begins to ask a new question:

How can I express the unique light within me?

This house governs:

- Creativity and artistic expression
- Romance and emotional passion
- Children and the act of creation
- Playfulness and joy
- Personal talents and gifts
- The courage to be seen

The Fifth House is where the soul begins to celebrate its individuality in a visible and heartfelt way.

The Spark of Creation

Creation is one of the most powerful forces within the universe.

- Stars create light.
- Nature creates forests and oceans.
- The human soul creates ideas, art, music, inventions, and relationships.

The Fifth House reflects this universal creative spark.

Here the soul begins to realize that it is not only a participant in life, it is also a creator within it.

Every painting, poem, invention, or inspired idea becomes a reflection of the soul's inner world.

Through creativity, the soul leaves its unique mark upon the Earth.

The Courage to Shine

Creative expression requires courage.

To share one's ideas or talents means allowing others to see a piece of the inner self.

Some souls feel naturally confident expressing themselves.

Others hesitate, fearing judgment or rejection.

Yet the Fifth House teaches that joy grows when we allow ourselves to be authentic.

When the soul shares its gifts freely, it inspires others to do the same.

In this way creativity becomes contagious, spreading inspiration from one heart to another.

The Joy of Play

The Fifth House also reminds the soul of something easily forgotten in adulthood:

play is essential to life.

Children naturally understand this truth.

They explore, imagine, and create without worrying about perfection.

Play allows the mind to relax and the spirit to expand.

Even in adulthood, moments of playfulness help restore balance and awaken fresh inspiration.

When the soul remembers how to play, life regains its sense of wonder.

The Experience of Romance

Romantic love also belongs to the Fifth House.

Through romance, the soul experiences excitement, attraction, and emotional connection.

These experiences awaken powerful feelings that reveal new aspects of the heart.

Romance teaches the soul about:

- Desire
- Admiration
- Vulnerability
- Passion

Some romantic experiences bring joy and inspiration.

Others bring lessons about expectations and emotional growth.

Yet every experience contributes to the soul's understanding of love.

Children and the Legacy of Creation

The Fifth House also governs children, both literal and symbolic.

For many souls, raising children becomes one of the most meaningful creative experiences of life.

Children represent the continuation of life itself.

But creation is not limited to biological offspring.

Art, music, writing, inventions, and ideas are also forms of children, expressions of the soul's creative energy that continue to influence the world long after they are created.

In this way the Fifth House reflects the soul's desire to leave something meaningful behind.

The Balance of Ego and Expression

Because the Fifth House involves personal expression, it also touches upon the concept of ego.

Ego is not inherently negative.

In its healthy form, ego allows the soul to feel pride in its accomplishments and confidence in its talents.

However, the soul must learn balance.

When creativity becomes motivated only by recognition or approval, joy may fade.

True creative fulfillment comes from the act of expression itself.

When the soul creates from love rather than ego, its gifts flow freely and inspire others.

The Soul's Lesson Here

The Fifth House teaches the soul several joyful truths:

- Creativity is a natural expression of the soul
- Joy is an essential part of life's journey
- Love awakens powerful emotional growth
- Authentic expression inspires others

Through these experiences, the soul learns that life is not only about survival or responsibility, it is also about celebration.

The Next Stage of Growth

After discovering creativity and joy, the soul begins to notice something else.

Life is not only about personal expression.

It is also about contribution.

The next stage of the journey introduces responsibility, service, and the refinement of personal abilities.

CHAPTER 44:
THE SOUL IN THE SIXTH HOUSE

The Path of Service

The Sixth House represents the stage where the soul begins to refine its talents and apply them in meaningful ways.

If the Fifth House asks, *"What can I create?"* the Sixth House asks a new question:

"How can I be useful?"

This house governs:

- Work and daily responsibilities
- Service to others
- Health and physical well-being
- Skill development
- Discipline and routine
- The refinement of personal abilities

The Sixth House reminds the soul that even the smallest acts of service contribute to the harmony of the greater world.

The Sacred Nature of Work

Many people think of work simply as a way to earn money.

But in the deeper language of the soul, work represents something much more profound.

Work is the process through which the soul applies its gifts to the world.

- A teacher shares knowledge.
- A gardener nurtures life.
- A doctor restores health.

- An artist brings beauty.

Each role contributes to the balance of human society.

The Sixth House teaches the soul that work is not merely an obligation; it can become a form of spiritual participation in the unfolding of life.

The Discipline of Growth

The Sixth House also introduces the soul to the concept of discipline.

Creativity alone is not enough to develop mastery.

Practice is required.
Effort is required.
Patience is required.

A musician must practice scales.
A writer must revise their work.
A healer must study the human body.

Through repetition and dedication, raw talent becomes skill.

The Sixth House reminds the soul that greatness often grows through daily effort rather than sudden inspiration.

Health and the Body

The Sixth House also governs physical health.

Here, the soul learns that the body is the vessel through which life is experienced.

Food, rest, movement, and balance become important elements of well-being.

When the body is cared for, the soul can express itself more fully.

Neglect of health can limit the soul's ability to pursue its purpose.

Thus, the Sixth House encourages the soul to develop awareness of its physical needs.

The body becomes not merely a biological form but a sacred instrument of life.

The Power of Small Actions

One of the most important lessons of the Sixth House is understanding the importance of small actions.

Grand achievements often begin with modest efforts repeated consistently over time.

A single act of kindness may brighten someone's entire day.

A small improvement in daily habits may lead to lasting health.

The Sixth House teaches the soul that greatness is not always dramatic.

Often, it appears quietly through consistency, care, and attention to detail.

Service and Humility

In the Fifth House, the soul experiences recognition and personal expression.

In the Sixth House, it learns humility.

Service means offering one's abilities without always expecting applause.

The soul begins to understand that helping others can bring deep fulfillment.

This realization transforms ordinary tasks into acts of compassion.

When work is performed with sincerity and kindness, it becomes an expression of love.

Healing as a Spiritual Path

Because the Sixth House is connected to service and health, it is often associated with healing professions.

Many souls feel called to help others recover from illness, emotional struggle, or hardship.

Yet healing does not belong only to doctors or therapists.

Anyone who offers comfort, understanding, or practical help participates in the healing of the world.

Through these experiences the soul discovers that compassion is one of the most powerful forces in existence.

The Soul's Lesson Here

The Sixth House teaches the soul several important truths:

- Every gift can be used in service to others
- Discipline transforms talent into mastery
- The body is a sacred instrument of life
- Small daily actions shape the larger journey

Through these lessons the soul learns responsibility and dedication.

Preparing for Deeper Relationships

As the soul learns to contribute through service, it begins to recognize something even more profound.

Life is not meant to be lived entirely alone.

After refining its abilities and learning responsibility, the soul becomes ready to explore deep partnership and cooperation with others.

CHAPTER 45: THE SOUL IN THE SEVENTH HOUSE

The Mirror of Relationship

The Seventh House represents the soul's encounter with partnership, cooperation, and reflection through others.

If the First House declares *"I am,"* the Seventh House introduces the realization:

"You are."

And through this recognition, the soul begins to understand that life is a dance between self and other.

This house governs:

- Marriage and romantic partnerships
- Business alliances
- Agreements and contracts
- Cooperation and diplomacy
- The ability to see oneself through another's eyes

The Seventh House teaches one of the most important spiritual truths:

- relationships are mirrors of the soul.

The Reflection of Self

When two people come together, something remarkable happens.

Each person becomes a mirror reflecting aspects of the other.

Through relationships we often see:

Our strengths
Our fears

Our habits
Our emotional patterns

Sometimes these reflections feel joyful and affirming.

At other times, they reveal parts of ourselves that we have avoided or misunderstood.

But every reflection carries an opportunity for growth.

The Seventh House reminds the soul that others are not obstacles; they are teachers.

The Desire for Partnership

Human beings naturally seek connection.

The Seventh House represents the soul's desire to share life with another person in meaningful ways.

Partnership can take many forms:

Marriage
Romantic relationships
Friendships
Business partnerships
Creative collaborations

Through these bonds, the soul learns how to balance independence with cooperation.

Partnership asks an important question:

How can two individuals walk together without losing themselves?

The Art of Balance

One of the greatest lessons of the Seventh House is balance.

Relationships require compromise, communication, and mutual respect.

Too much independence may create distance.

Too much dependence may create an imbalance.

Healthy relationships allow both individuals to grow while supporting one another's journeys.

Through this process, the soul learns that true partnership does not limit freedom; it enhances it.

Love as a Teacher

Romantic love often becomes the most powerful classroom of the Seventh House.

Love can bring joy, inspiration, and a deep emotional connection.

But it can also reveal vulnerabilities and hidden fears.

When conflicts arise, they often highlight areas where the soul still needs healing or understanding.

Through these experiences, the soul learns patience, empathy, forgiveness, and compassion.

In this way, love becomes a teacher guiding the soul toward emotional maturity.

Agreements and Commitment

The Seventh House also governs agreements and commitments.

When two people enter a partnership, they create a shared path.

Commitment requires trust.

It requires honesty.

It requires the willingness to support one another through both easy and difficult times.

The soul learns that promises are sacred bonds that shape the course of life.

Honoring commitments strengthens integrity and deepens connection.

Learning Through Contrast

Not every relationship is easy.

Some relationships challenge us deeply.

They may reveal emotional wounds, insecurities, or patterns we did not realize we carried.

While these experiences may feel painful at times, they often contain the greatest opportunities for growth.

Through contrast, the soul becomes aware of what it truly needs and values.

In this way even difficult relationships contribute to spiritual understanding.

The Soul's Lesson Here

The Seventh House teaches several profound truths:

- Relationships reveal who we truly are
- Partnership requires balance between independence and cooperation
- Love encourages emotional growth and compassion

Commitment strengthens integrity and trust

Through these lessons the soul learns that connection is one of the most powerful forces shaping human experience.

The Gateway to Transformation

As the soul explores partnership, it eventually discovers that relationships can open the door to even deeper experiences.

Beyond companionship lies the realm of shared transformation.

This next stage leads into the mysterious and powerful territory of the Eighth House.

CHAPTER 46: THE SOUL IN THE EIGHTH HOUSE

The Chamber of Transformation

The Eighth House represents the realm of deep change, emotional intensity, and spiritual rebirth.

If the Seventh House teaches the soul about partnership, the Eighth House teaches what happens when those partnerships bring profound transformation.

This house governs:

- Intimacy and emotional vulnerability
- Shared resources and financial partnerships
- Psychological depth
- Endings and new beginnings
- Death and rebirth symbolism
- The mysteries of life

The Eighth House is often misunderstood because it deals with subjects many people find uncomfortable.

Yet it is one of the most powerful houses in the chart, because it reveals where the soul learns to shed old identities and emerge renewed.

The Power of Emotional Depth

In earlier stages of life, the soul may keep certain emotions hidden.

Fear, grief, jealousy, or vulnerability may remain beneath the surface.

The Eighth House invites the soul to face these hidden feelings.

Rather than avoiding emotional depth, the soul begins to explore it.

Through this exploration, the soul gains psychological insight and emotional strength.

Understanding one's inner world becomes a key to transformation.

Intimacy and Trust

The Eighth House is closely associated with intimacy.

While the Seventh House teaches partnership, the Eighth House teaches complete emotional sharing.

Intimacy requires trust.

It involves revealing parts of ourselves that are rarely shown to others.

This vulnerability can feel frightening, yet it also creates the possibility for profound connection.

When two souls share their deepest truths, a powerful bond is formed.

Through such experiences, the soul learns that authentic connection requires honesty and courage.

The Cycle of Endings and Beginnings

One of the most important lessons of the Eighth House is understanding that life moves through cycles.

Some chapters must end so that new ones can begin.

Relationships may change.
Careers may shift.
Old beliefs may dissolve.

While these transitions may feel difficult, they are often necessary for growth.

The Eighth House reminds the soul that transformation is a natural part of life's evolution.

Just as a snake sheds its skin or a phoenix rises from ashes, the soul continually renews itself.

Shared Resources

The Eighth House also governs shared financial and material resources.

This includes inheritance, investments, or financial partnerships.

Through these experiences, the soul learns lessons about trust, responsibility, and cooperation.

Money in the Eighth House often reflects deeper emotional dynamics.

Power struggles, generosity, or mutual support may appear depending on how individuals approach shared resources.

Ultimately, the lesson involves learning how to manage shared power wisely.

The Mystery of Death and Rebirth

Symbolically, the Eighth House represents death, not only physical death but also the ending of old identities.

Throughout life, the soul undergoes many symbolic deaths.

Old versions of ourselves disappear as we grow into new awareness.

A shy child may become a confident adult.

A painful experience may transform into wisdom.

Each transformation is a form of rebirth.

The Eighth House teaches that death and rebirth are not opposites; they are two parts of the same cycle.

Discovering Inner Power

As the soul moves through Eighth House experiences, it begins to discover something remarkable:

true power comes from transformation.

When the soul confronts its fears, heals emotional wounds, and embraces change, it becomes stronger and wiser.

The struggles of the Eighth House often reveal hidden resilience.

Through transformation, the soul discovers abilities it never knew it possessed.

The Soul's Lesson Here

The Eighth House teaches several profound truths:

- Emotional honesty leads to a deeper connection
- Transformation is necessary for growth
- Endings often prepare the way for new beginnings
- Inner strength is discovered through facing challenges

Through these lessons, the soul learns that change, though sometimes painful, is often the gateway to profound renewal.

The Rising of Wisdom

After experiencing the powerful transformations of the Eighth House, the soul begins to seek meaning in these experiences.

Questions naturally arise:

Why did these events occur?
What wisdom can be gained from them?
How does life fit into a larger purpose?

CHAPTER 47:
THE SOUL IN THE NINTH HOUSE

The Search for Meaning

The Ninth House represents the soul's quest for truth, wisdom, and a larger understanding of life.

After passing through the deep emotional transformations of the Eighth House, the soul begins to look upward and outward. It seeks answers beyond immediate circumstances.

Here, the soul asks profound questions:

Why am I here?
What is the meaning of life?
What truths govern the universe?

The Ninth House governs:

- Philosophy and spiritual belief
- Higher education and wisdom
- Travel and cultural exploration
- Religious or spiritual traditions
- Personal belief systems
- The expansion of the mind

This house invites the soul to explore the world not only through experience, but through understanding.

The Desire for Knowledge

While the Third House introduced curiosity and basic learning, the Ninth House seeks higher wisdom.

This is the stage where the soul begins to explore larger frameworks of knowledge.

Universities, spiritual teachings, philosophical writings, and sacred texts all belong to this realm.

The soul becomes fascinated with questions that stretch beyond daily life.

Instead of asking how something works, the soul now asks:

What is the deeper truth behind existence?

This search often leads individuals into fields such as philosophy, theology, law, science, or cultural studies.

Travel as a Teacher

Travel is also closely associated with the Ninth House.

When the soul encounters new lands, cultures, and traditions, it begins to realize how vast and diverse the world truly is.

Travel expands awareness.

A person raised in one culture may discover entirely different ways of living and thinking when they explore another.

Through these experiences, the soul learns humility and appreciation for humanity's diversity.

Every journey becomes a classroom where the soul gathers new perspectives.

The Formation of Belief

The Ninth House also governs belief systems.

Throughout life, each soul develops a personal philosophy, a way of understanding the universe and one's place within it.

Some people inherit religious traditions from family.

Others explore many spiritual paths before discovering what resonates with their inner truth.

The important lesson of the Ninth House is that beliefs must grow through experience and reflection, not blind acceptance.

The soul must examine its beliefs carefully, ensuring that they bring wisdom rather than limitation.

Faith and Hope

The Ninth House introduces the concept of faith.

Faith does not necessarily require certainty.

Rather, it is the willingness to trust that life has purpose, even when its meaning is not immediately clear.

Faith provides courage during difficult times.

It allows the soul to move forward with hope rather than fear.

Whether expressed through religion, spirituality, philosophy, or personal conviction, faith becomes a guiding light for the journey ahead.

Teaching and Sharing Wisdom

Once the soul gains knowledge and insight, a natural desire often arises to share that wisdom with others.

Teachers, writers, philosophers, and spiritual guides all operate within the realm of the Ninth House.

Through teaching, the soul passes knowledge forward, helping others grow in understanding.

This sharing of wisdom becomes part of humanity's collective evolution.

Every insight offered contributes to the unfolding story of human awareness.

The Soul's Lesson Here

The Ninth House teaches the soul several powerful truths:

- Wisdom grows through exploration and experience
- Truth must be discovered personally
- Cultural and spiritual diversity expands understanding
- Faith can guide the soul through uncertainty

Through these lessons, the soul begins to see life as part of a much greater journey.

From Wisdom to Purpose

After seeking knowledge and truth, the soul begins to ask another important question:

How can I apply this wisdom in the world?

Understanding alone is not enough.

The soul now feels called to build something meaningful and lasting.

CHAPTER 48:
THE SOUL IN THE TENTH HOUSE

The Path of Purpose

The Tenth House represents the stage where the soul steps forward into the wider world to fulfill its public role and life purpose.

If the Fourth House reflects our roots and private life, the Tenth House represents our contribution to society.

It is the highest point in the birth chart, often associated with the Midheaven, symbolizing visibility, responsibility, and achievement.

The Tenth House governs:

- Career and professional direction
- Leadership and authority
- Reputation and public image
- Long-term achievements
- Responsibility and legacy

Here, the soul begins asking one of life's most meaningful questions:

What am I meant to accomplish in this lifetime?

The Call to Responsibility

As the soul matures, it begins to understand that life offers opportunities to influence the world in meaningful ways.

The Tenth House invites the soul to step beyond personal interests and take responsibility for something greater than itself.

For some people this calling appears through career.

For others it may appear through community leadership, creative contributions, or guiding others with wisdom and compassion.

Regardless of the form it takes, the Tenth House represents the soul's effort to leave a lasting impact.

The Role of Ambition

Ambition often plays an important role in the Tenth House.

Ambition is the desire to reach higher, to build something meaningful, and to realize one's potential.

However, ambition must be guided by integrity.

When ambition is motivated only by power or recognition, it may lead the soul away from its deeper purpose.

But when ambition arises from a genuine desire to contribute, it becomes a powerful force for positive change.

The Tenth House teaches that true success is not measured only by status but by the value of one's contributions to the world.

Leadership and Influence

The Tenth House is also associated with leadership.

Some individuals are called to guide organizations, communities, or even nations.

Others lead through quiet influence, mentoring others, teaching wisdom, or setting an example through their actions.

Leadership does not always require public attention.

Sometimes the most meaningful leadership occurs when a person inspires others simply by living with honesty, compassion, and courage.

The soul learns that leadership is not about control, it is about responsibility and service.

Reputation and Legacy

Another important aspect of the Tenth House is reputation.

How others perceive us in the world often reflects our actions and values.

Reputation is built slowly over time through consistent behavior.

Integrity, honesty, and dedication create respect and trust.

The soul eventually realizes that reputation is not about impressing others but about living in alignment with one's highest principles.

This alignment shapes the legacy we leave behind.

The Meaning of Legacy

Legacy is the imprint a life leaves upon the world.

Some legacies are visible through achievements, inventions, or leadership.

Others appear through kindness, wisdom, and the lives we influence.

A teacher may inspire generations of students.

A parent may shape the future through nurturing a child's potential.

A writer may share ideas that continue to inspire long after their lifetime.

The Tenth House reminds us that every life contributes something meaningful to the human story.

The Balance Between Public and Private Life

While the Tenth House focuses on public achievement, the soul must remember the importance of balance.

Ambition without emotional grounding can lead to exhaustion or isolation.

The Fourth House, the opposite of the Tenth, reminds us to maintain connection with family, inner peace, and emotional well-being.

When these two houses remain balanced, the soul can pursue purpose without losing its humanity.

The Soul's Lesson Here

The Tenth House teaches several profound truths:

- Every soul has a purpose to fulfill
- Responsibility brings maturity and strength
- Leadership requires integrity and compassion
- Legacy is created through meaningful contribution

Through these lessons, the soul learns that life is not only about personal experience, it is also about participating in the greater story of humanity.

The Next Stage of the Journey

After stepping into purpose and responsibility, the soul begins to recognize something even larger.

Its efforts are not isolated.

They are part of a greater network of people working together to shape the future.

CHAPTER 49:
THE SOUL IN THE ELEVENTH HOUSE

The Circle of Humanity

The Eleventh House represents the soul's connection with community, friendship, and collective vision.

If the Tenth House asks, *"What is my purpose?"* the Eleventh House asks a new question:

"How can my purpose contribute to the greater good?"

This house governs:

- Friendships and social connections
- Communities and organizations
- Humanitarian efforts
- Collective goals and shared dreams
- Innovation and progress
- The future of humanity

Here, the soul begins to understand that individual lives are threads woven into a much larger tapestry.

The Meaning of Friendship

Friendships play an important role in the Eleventh House.

Unlike family relationships that are formed through birth, friendships are chosen connections.

These relationships often reflect shared values, interests, and dreams.

Through friendships, the soul experiences companionship, support, and mutual growth.

Friends often inspire us to become better versions of ourselves.

They remind us that life is not meant to be traveled alone.

The Power of Community

The Eleventh House also represents communities and groups working toward common goals.

Throughout history, communities have shaped the direction of human progress.

Scientific discoveries, social movements, and cultural innovations often emerge when individuals join together with a shared vision.

When people unite for positive purposes, their combined efforts create powerful change.

The soul learns that cooperation multiplies the strength of individual contributions.

Shared Dreams for the Future

The Eleventh House is closely connected to the future.

It represents hopes, aspirations, and visions for a better world.

Many individuals with strong Eleventh House influences feel drawn toward improving society.

They may participate in humanitarian efforts, social reform, environmental protection, or technological innovation.

These dreams are not merely personal desires.

They reflect the soul's recognition that humanity itself is evolving.

Each generation builds upon the efforts of those who came before.

Innovation and Progress

The Eleventh House is also associated with innovation.

New ideas often arise when individuals question old assumptions and imagine new possibilities.

Inventors, scientists, visionaries, and reformers often carry strong Eleventh House energy.

Their willingness to explore unconventional ideas opens pathways for human advancement.

Yet innovation must be guided by wisdom and compassion.

True progress benefits not only individuals but the entire human family.

The Balance Between Individuality and Unity

The Eleventh House teaches an important balance.

While community is valuable, individuality must still be honored.

Each person brings unique gifts to the collective.

When individuality is suppressed, creativity fades.

When individuality is respected, diversity becomes a strength.

The soul learns that the most harmonious communities are those where individuals contribute their unique talents while supporting one another's growth.

Humanity as a Living Network

One of the most inspiring lessons of the Eleventh House is the realization that humanity functions as a living network.

Ideas travel across continents.

Acts of kindness ripple outward through countless lives.

A single discovery can influence generations.

Every soul contributes to this network in some way.

Through friendship, collaboration, and shared vision, the human family gradually evolves toward greater understanding.

The Soul's Lesson Here

The Eleventh House teaches several powerful truths:

- Friendship and cooperation strengthen the human journey
- Shared goals create collective progress
- Innovation opens new possibilities for humanity
- Individual gifts contribute to the greater good

Through these lessons, the soul begins to see life from a wider perspective.

The individual journey expands into a collective one.

The Final Stage of the Journey

After experiencing connection with humanity, the soul begins to sense something even greater.

Beyond community lies the awareness that all existence is interconnected.

CHAPTER 50:
THE SOUL IN THE TWELFTH HOUSE

Returning to the Infinite

The Twelfth House is the final stage of the soul's journey through the zodiac.

It represents the realm of mystery, spiritual awareness, compassion, and the dissolution of the ego.

If the First House begins with the declaration *"I am,"* the Twelfth House softly whispers another truth:

"I am part of everything."

Here, the boundaries that once defined identity begin to soften. The soul realizes that life has always been part of a greater unfolding.

The Twelfth House governs:

- Spiritual awakening
- Compassion and forgiveness
- Hidden dimensions of consciousness
- Dreams and intuition
- Solitude and reflection
- The completion of karmic cycles

It is often called the house of transcendence, because it allows the soul to move beyond ordinary perception and glimpse the unity that connects all life.

The Dissolution of the Ego

Throughout life, the ego helps us navigate the physical world. It defines identity, protects individuality, and guides personal ambitions.

Yet the Twelfth House teaches that identity is not limited to the roles we play.

We are more than our achievements.

We are more than our struggles.

We are more than the stories we tell about ourselves.

In the quiet spaces of reflection, the soul begins to see beyond these temporary identities.

This realization does not erase individuality; it simply places it within a larger spiritual context.

The soul begins to recognize that life is both deeply personal and universally connected.

The Power of Compassion

One of the most beautiful expressions of the Twelfth House is compassion.

When the soul sees beyond separation, it begins to understand the suffering and joy of others as part of a shared human experience.

Compassion is not weakness.

It is a strength born from understanding.

Those who embody Twelfth House wisdom often feel called to help others.

They may work in healing professions, spiritual guidance, humanitarian efforts, or simply live lives devoted to kindness and service.

These individuals recognize that helping another soul is also a way of healing themselves.

The Realm of Dreams and Intuition

The Twelfth House is closely connected to the subconscious mind.

Dreams, intuition, and subtle perceptions often emerge more strongly here.

While the physical senses perceive the outer world, intuition allows the soul to perceive deeper truths.

Many spiritual traditions teach that dreams can act as messages from the deeper layers of consciousness.

They may reflect unresolved emotions, spiritual insights, or symbolic guidance for life's journey.

When we learn to listen to these inner signals, we gain access to a form of wisdom that cannot always be explained through logic alone.

Solitude and Sacred Reflection

The Twelfth House often invites periods of solitude.

This solitude is not meant to isolate the soul from the world, but to allow space for reflection and spiritual renewal.

Throughout history, many philosophers, mystics, artists, and visionaries have spent time in quiet contemplation.

In solitude, distractions fade.

The mind becomes calmer.

The deeper voice of the soul can finally be heard.

Moments of silence often reveal insights that cannot be discovered through constant activity.

The Completion of Karmic Cycles

Another powerful theme of the Twelfth House is completion.

Life experiences accumulate wisdom over time.

Every joy and every hardship contributes to the soul's growth.

The Twelfth House represents the closing of a cycle.

Here the soul reflects on the lessons learned throughout the journey.

Patterns that once created suffering may finally be understood and released.

Forgiveness becomes possible, not only for others but also for oneself.

Through forgiveness, the soul frees itself from the weight of the past.

This liberation prepares the soul for renewal.

The Gateway to Renewal

Although the Twelfth House represents endings, it is not an ending in the traditional sense.

It is a doorway.

Just as the seasons move in cycles, the soul continues evolving through many stages of existence.

When the soul releases old identities, old fears, and old wounds, it creates space for something new to emerge.

This renewal leads naturally back to the beginning of the zodiac.

From the quiet wisdom of the Twelfth House, the soul once again approaches the spark of the First House, where identity is reborn with deeper understanding.

The Great Realization

The greatest lesson of the Twelfth House is the realization that separation is an illusion.

The soul is not isolated.

It is part of a vast and interconnected universe.
Every life contributes to the unfolding story of existence.
Every act of kindness strengthens the web of humanity.
Every moment of awareness brings the soul closer to truth.
When the soul understands this, fear begins to dissolve.
In its place emerges peace.

The Soul's Final Lesson

The Twelfth House teaches that the ultimate purpose of life is not domination, accumulation, or recognition.

The true purpose is awakening.
To awaken to compassion.
To awaken to wisdom.
To awaken to unity.

When the soul understands this, the journey through the zodiac becomes more than a sequence of experiences.

It becomes a sacred path of growth, awareness, and love.

The Cycle Continues

As the Twelfth House closes the circle, a new beginning waits quietly beyond the horizon.

From the stillness of completion, the soul gathers its wisdom and prepares to begin again.

With new insight.

With deeper compassion.

With a clearer understanding of its place in the universe.

And so the eternal journey continues.

PART V:

READING THE SOUL MAP

CHAPTER 51:
READING THE SOUL MAP

How the Signs and Houses Work Together

By now, you have traveled through the twelve signs and the twelve houses.

You have seen how the zodiac reveals the personality of the soul, and how the houses reveal the areas of life where that personality unfolds.

But astrology becomes truly powerful when these two elements are brought together.

The sign describes the nature of the energy.

The house describes where that energy expresses itself.

Together, they form what can be called the Soul Map, a blueprint of how a person experiences life, growth, relationships, purpose, and spiritual evolution.

Understanding this map allows us to see ourselves more clearly and navigate life with greater wisdom.

The Signs as the Soul's Personality

The zodiac signs describe the style in which the soul expresses itself.

Each sign carries a unique vibration and perspective.

For example:

- Aries expresses courage and initiative.
- Taurus expresses stability and patience.
- Gemini expresses curiosity and communication.
- Cancer expresses emotional connection and nurturing.
- Leo expresses creativity and leadership.

- Virgo expresses service and refinement.
- Libra expresses balance and partnership.
- Scorpio expresses transformation and depth.
- Sagittarius expresses exploration and truth.
- Capricorn expresses discipline and achievement.
- Aquarius expresses innovation and vision.
- Pisces expresses compassion and spiritual awareness.

These energies do not exist in isolation.

Each person contains all twelve signs within their birth chart, each influencing different aspects of life.

The Houses as the Soul's Life Experiences

While the signs describe energy, the houses describe experience.

Each house represents an area of life where the soul learns lessons and gains understanding.

The First House reveals identity.

The Second House explores value and resources.

The Third House develops communication and thought.

The Fourth House connects us to home and emotional roots.

The Fifth House awakens creativity and joy.

The Sixth House teaches service and discipline.

The Seventh House explores relationships and partnerships.

The Eighth House invites transformation and deep emotional change.

The Ninth House seeks wisdom and philosophical understanding.

The Tenth House reveals life purpose and contribution to society.

The Eleventh House connects the soul to community and collective vision.

The Twelfth House invites spiritual awakening and completion.

Each house represents a stage of experience that shapes the soul's development.

The Meeting of Energy and Experience

When a sign occupies a house in the birth chart, the qualities of that sign influence how the soul approaches that area of life.

For example:

If Aries occupies the First House, the individual may appear bold, confident, and direct.

If Taurus occupies the Second House, the individual may value stability and security in financial matters.

If Gemini occupies the Third House, communication may come naturally, and curiosity may guide learning.

These combinations create the unique patterns that make every individual different.

No two birth charts are exactly alike.

Even people born on the same day may experience life differently because of subtle variations in planetary placement.

The Soul's Unique Design

The birth chart can be compared to a musical composition.

The zodiac signs are like musical tones.

The houses are like instruments.

The planets act as musicians playing the notes.

Together, they create the symphony of a human life.

Some lives are quiet and reflective.

Others are bold and adventurous.

Some focus on creativity, while others focus on service or discovery.

None is better or worse.

They are simply different expressions of the same universal intelligence.

Astrology as Self-Understanding

Astrology is not meant to place limits on people.

It is meant to offer insight.

When we understand the patterns influencing our lives, we can make more conscious choices.

We begin to recognize our strengths.

We also become aware of habits that may hold us back.

With awareness comes the ability to grow.

The birth chart does not control destiny.

It simply reveals the landscape through which the soul travels.

The Living Map

A Soul Map is not static.

Life experiences continually shape how the energies of the chart express themselves.

As people mature, they often learn to balance the different parts of their personality.

A shy child may grow into a confident adult.

A person who once struggled with fear may discover courage through experience.

The chart remains the same, but the soul's understanding evolves.

The Invitation of the Soul Map

The true purpose of understanding the Soul Map is not prediction.

It is self-awareness.

When individuals understand their own patterns, they can move through life with greater clarity.

They can develop their talents, heal emotional wounds, and align themselves with their deeper purpose.

Astrology becomes a mirror reflecting the deeper nature of the soul.

Through that reflection, the journey of life becomes more meaningful.

The Next Step

Now that we understand how the signs and houses work together, the next step is to explore the role of the planets.

The planets represent the forces that activate the energies of the chart.

They show how the soul thinks, feels, acts, and evolves through experience.

Understanding the planets adds another layer of depth to the Soul Map.

CHAPTER 52:
THE PLANETS

Messengers of the Soul

If the zodiac signs are the language of the soul and the houses are the stages where life unfolds, the planets are the messengers that carry the soul's intentions into action.

They represent the moving forces within the human experience, the impulses that guide our thoughts, emotions, desires, and spiritual growth.

Each planet symbolizes a different aspect of consciousness. Together they create a complex and beautiful system that reveals how the soul interacts with the world.

The ancient astrologers often referred to the planets as celestial teachers, because each one offers lessons that help shape the human journey.

Understanding the planets allows us to see not only *who we are*, but also how we grow.

The Inner and Outer Planets

Astrology traditionally divides the planets into two groups.

The inner planets influence our personal personality and everyday experiences.

The outer planets represent deeper evolutionary forces that shape generations and collective transformation.

The inner planets move quickly through the zodiac, reflecting our daily thoughts, feelings, and actions.

The outer planets move slowly, influencing entire periods of history and the evolution of human consciousness.

Both are essential in understanding the full map of the soul.

The Sun

The Center of Identity

Although technically a star rather than a planet, the Sun holds the most central role in astrology.

It represents the core identity of the soul.

The Sun reveals our sense of purpose, vitality, and creative expression. It is the light within us that seeks to shine and express itself fully.

Just as the Sun gives life to the solar system, the Sun in the birth chart represents the energy that fuels personal growth and self-realization.

The journey of life often involves discovering how to express the Sun's qualities in a healthy and balanced way.

The Moon

The Emotional Soul

The Moon represents our emotional nature and inner world.

It governs instinct, memory, and our deepest sense of security.

While the Sun shows who we strive to become, the Moon reflects the emotional patterns we carry from early life experiences.

It is closely connected to family, nurturing, and the need to feel safe and understood.

The Moon reminds us that emotional awareness is essential for spiritual growth.

When we understand our emotional patterns, we gain the ability to heal and transform them.

Mercury

The Mind and Communication

Mercury represents thought, language, and the exchange of ideas.

It governs how we learn, process information, and communicate with others.

A strong Mercury placement often indicates curiosity, intelligence, and adaptability.

Mercury teaches the importance of listening as well as speaking.

Communication is one of the primary tools through which humans share knowledge and build relationships.

Through Mercury, the soul learns to translate inner awareness into meaningful dialogue with the world.

Venus

Love, Beauty, and Harmony

Venus represents attraction, affection, and the appreciation of beauty.

It governs relationships, artistic expression, and the values that guide our choices.

Venus reminds us that life is not only about survival or achievement.

It is also about joy, pleasure, and emotional connection.

Through Venus, we learn the importance of kindness, cooperation, and the ability to appreciate the beauty that surrounds us.

Healthy Venus energy encourages harmony in relationships and encourages us to value ourselves and others.

Mars

Energy and Courage

Mars represents action, ambition, and determination.

It governs our ability to assert ourselves and pursue goals with confidence.

Mars is the driving force that pushes us to overcome obstacles and take initiative.

However, Mars must be balanced with wisdom.

When expressed without awareness, it can lead to conflict or impulsive decisions.

When expressed with maturity, Mars becomes the energy of courage, leadership, and constructive change.

Jupiter

Expansion and Wisdom

Jupiter symbolizes growth, opportunity, and philosophical understanding.

It is often associated with good fortune, but its deeper meaning is expansion of awareness.

Jupiter encourages exploration, education, travel, and spiritual discovery.

It invites us to broaden our perspective and seek truth beyond our immediate surroundings.

Through Jupiter, the soul learns optimism, faith, and the importance of believing in possibilities.

Saturn

Discipline and Mastery

Saturn represents structure, responsibility, and life lessons.

It is sometimes called the teacher of the zodiac because it reveals the areas where we must develop patience and perseverance.

While Saturn may appear restrictive at times, its purpose is not punishment.

Its purpose is maturity.

Saturn teaches that lasting success comes from dedication, effort, and the willingness to learn from challenges.

The lessons of Saturn often become the foundation of wisdom later in life.

Uranus

Awakening and Innovation

Uranus represents sudden change, originality, and the breaking of old patterns.

It is associated with invention, freedom, and revolutionary ideas.

When Uranus is active in a chart, it often signals periods of awakening where old beliefs are replaced by new insights.

Uranus encourages individuals to question tradition and explore new possibilities.

Through this planet, the soul learns that progress often requires courage to think differently.

Neptune

Spiritual Vision

Neptune governs imagination, intuition, and spiritual awareness.

It dissolves boundaries and encourages compassion, creativity, and mystical understanding.

Neptune can inspire art, music, and profound spiritual experiences.

However, its energy can also create confusion if not grounded in reality.

The lesson of Neptune is to balance dreams with clarity, allowing inspiration to guide life without losing practical awareness.

Pluto

Transformation and Rebirth

Pluto represents the deepest forces of transformation.

It governs the cycles of death and rebirth that occur throughout life.

Pluto's influence often brings profound change, forcing individuals to confront hidden fears, emotional wounds, and psychological patterns.

Although these experiences can be intense, they ultimately lead to renewal.

Pluto reminds us that true growth often emerges from the courage to face the darkest corners of our inner world.

Through transformation comes empowerment.

The Living Symphony of the Planets

When these planetary energies interact within the birth chart, they create a living symphony of human experience.

Each person carries a unique combination of planetary influences.

Some lives emphasize creativity.

Others emphasize leadership, compassion, or discovery.

The planets reveal the dynamic forces that shape personality, relationships, and life direction.

Understanding these energies allows individuals to work with them consciously rather than feeling controlled by unseen forces.

The Soul's Teachers

Every planet represents a teacher.

The Sun teaches identity.

The Moon teaches emotional awareness.
Mercury teaches communication.
Venus teaches love.
Mars teaches courage.
Jupiter teaches wisdom.
Saturn teaches discipline.
Uranus teaches awakening.
Neptune teaches spiritual vision.
Pluto teaches transformation.

Together, they guide the soul through the many stages of growth and understanding.

The Next Layer of the Soul Map

Now that we understand the roles of the planets, the next layer of astrology reveals how these planetary energies interact with one another.

These interactions are known as aspects.

Aspects reveal the relationships between planetary forces and show how different parts of the personality cooperate, or sometimes challenge one another.

CHAPTER 53:
ASPECTS

The Conversations Between the Planets

If the planets are the messengers of the soul, the aspects are the conversations they have with one another.

These conversations create the dynamic patterns that shape personality, behavior, and life experience.

In a birth chart, the planets form angles with one another across the zodiac. Each of these angles carries a specific type of energy that influences how the planetary forces interact.

Some aspects create harmony and ease.

Others create tension and challenge.

Both types are essential for growth.

Without harmony, life would feel like a constant struggle.

Without challenge, growth would rarely occur.

The aspects create the living dialogue that shapes the unfolding journey of the soul.

The Geometry of the Heavens

Astrology is deeply connected to sacred geometry.

The circle of the zodiac contains 360 degrees, and the aspects are formed when planets align at specific points within this circle.

These geometric relationships create patterns that astrologers have studied for thousands of years.

Each aspect reflects a different type of interaction between planetary energies.

Some allow the planets to cooperate easily.

Others create friction that pushes the soul to develop strength, patience, and awareness.

Understanding aspects allows us to see how the different parts of the personality either support one another or create internal tension.

Conjunction

The Blending of Energies

The conjunction occurs when two planets occupy the same degree or very close degrees in the zodiac.

In this aspect, the energies of the planets merge together.

Rather than acting separately, the planets combine their qualities into a single powerful influence.

For example, a conjunction between Mercury and Venus might create a person who communicates with grace and artistic sensitivity.

A conjunction between Mars and Jupiter may create tremendous enthusiasm and bold action.

The conjunction is powerful because it concentrates energy in one place.

However, the soul must learn how to balance the combined forces so that one does not overpower the other.

Sextile

Opportunity and Cooperation

The sextile occurs when two planets are approximately 60 degrees apart.

This aspect creates cooperation and opportunity.

The energies of the planets work together in supportive ways, encouraging growth and creativity.

Sextiles often bring talents that can develop naturally if the individual chooses to cultivate them.

Unlike the trine, which often flows effortlessly, the sextile still requires conscious participation.

When individuals actively engage these energies, they often discover hidden abilities and new possibilities.

Square

Growth Through Challenge

The square occurs when two planets form a 90-degree angle.

This aspect creates tension and conflict between planetary energies.

At first glance, squares may seem difficult or negative.

However, they are often the greatest engines of personal growth.

Squares force the soul to confront obstacles, develop discipline, and find creative solutions to life's challenges.

Many successful individuals have strong squares in their charts because these aspects push them to overcome limitations and reach their full potential.

The square teaches perseverance and resilience.

Trine

Natural Harmony

The trine occurs when planets form a 120-degree angle.

This aspect is associated with ease, harmony, and natural flow.

The energies of the planets support each other effortlessly.

Talents connected to trines often feel natural and instinctive.

However, the ease of the trine can sometimes lead to complacency if the individual does not actively develop these gifts.

When used consciously, trines provide powerful creative ability and emotional balance.

They represent the areas where life feels most aligned with the soul's natural rhythm.

Opposition

The Balance of Opposites

The opposition occurs when planets stand 180 degrees apart on the zodiac wheel.

This aspect represents polarity and balance.

Oppositions often manifest through relationships or external circumstances.

The soul may experience situations where two opposing forces must be reconciled.

For example, one planet may represent independence while the other represents partnership.

Through these experiences, individuals learn the importance of balance.

Oppositions teach that life is rarely one-sided.

Wisdom emerges when opposing energies are integrated rather than rejected.

Minor Aspects

In addition to the major aspects, astrologers also recognize several minor aspects that add subtle complexity to the birth chart.

These include:

- Semi-sextiles
- Quincunxes
- Sesquiquadrates
- Semi-squares

Although less dramatic than the major aspects, these relationships still influence personality and behavior.

They often represent subtle adjustments that the soul must make in order to maintain harmony within the chart.

The Dance of Energies

When all aspects are considered together, the birth chart becomes a complex and beautiful web of relationships.

Each planetary interaction contributes to the unfolding story of a life.

Some aspects create ease and natural talent.

Others create inner conflict that pushes the soul toward transformation.

Both are valuable.

The birth chart is not meant to describe perfection.

It describes potential.

Through awareness, individuals can learn to work with their strengths and grow through their challenges.

Aspects as Teachers

Each aspect offers a different lesson.

Conjunction teaches integration.

Sextile teaches opportunity.

Square teaches strength.

Trine teaches flow.

Opposition teaches balance.

Together, they shape the personality and guide the soul's development through experience.

By understanding these interactions, individuals gain deeper insight into the patterns that influence their lives.

The Soul's Evolving Pattern

As life unfolds, the planetary energies continue interacting through transits and progressions.

These movements activate the aspects in the birth chart, bringing new experiences and opportunities for growth.

Astrology, therefore, becomes not only a map of personality but also a map of evolution.

The soul is constantly learning, adjusting, and expanding its awareness.

The Next Step

The final step in understanding the Soul Map is learning how to bring all of these elements together.

The signs, houses, planets, and aspects combine to create the unique pattern that defines an individual's life path.

When interpreted together, they reveal the deeper purpose behind the soul’s journey.

CHAPTER 54: THE SOUL'S BLUEPRINT

Interpreting the Birth Chart

A birth chart is often called a map of the heavens at the moment of birth.

Yet in a deeper sense, it is something far more meaningful.

It is a blueprint of the soul's design for this lifetime.

At the exact moment a person enters the world, the positions of the planets create a symbolic pattern in the sky. This pattern becomes a reflection of the energetic influences shaping the individual's life path.

Astrology does not suggest that the planets control our lives.

Rather, they mirror the timing and pattern of the soul's unfolding journey.

Just as a seed contains the blueprint for the tree it will one day become, the birth chart contains the symbolic blueprint of the soul's growth and evolution.

The Four Foundations of the Chart

To understand a birth chart fully, four essential components must be considered together.

These are:

- The Signs
- The Houses
- The Planets
- The Aspects

Each element reveals a different dimension of the soul's experience.

When viewed together, they form a complex but beautiful picture of a person's inner nature and life direction.

The Signs: The Style of the Soul

The zodiac signs describe how energy expresses itself.

They represent the personality traits, emotional tendencies, and natural inclinations that shape behavior.

For example:

A person with strong Aries energy may approach life boldly and directly.

Someone influenced strongly by Pisces may be more intuitive, compassionate, and spiritually aware.

The signs describe the style in which the soul experiences life.

The Houses: The Areas of Life

While the signs describe personality qualities, the houses reveal where these energies appear in life.

Each house governs a different area of human experience.

Identity, relationships, career, creativity, spirituality, and emotional foundations all correspond to specific houses.

The houses show where the soul encounters its greatest opportunities for learning and growth.

For example, a strong influence in the Tenth House may emphasize public achievement and leadership, while a strong Twelfth House influence may emphasize spiritual awareness and introspection.

The Planets: The Forces of Action

The planets represent the active forces operating within the personality.

Each planet governs a specific function within the human experience.

The Sun represents identity and vitality.

The Moon governs emotional patterns.

Mercury shapes communication and thought.

Venus governs relationships and values.

Mars drives ambition and action.

Jupiter expands awareness and opportunity.

Saturn teaches discipline and responsibility.

Uranus awakens innovation and change.

Neptune inspires spirituality and imagination.

Pluto brings deep transformation.

These planetary energies act like actors within the soul's story, each playing an important role.

The Aspects: The Relationships Between Forces

The aspects reveal how the planetary energies interact with one another.

Some energies support each other easily.

Others create tension that pushes the soul to grow.

These interactions create the unique psychological pattern that shapes an individual's behavior and experiences.

In many ways, aspects reveal the inner dialogue of the personality.

They show where harmony exists and where lessons must be learned.

Reading the Whole Pattern

Interpreting a birth chart is much like observing a painting.

Each brushstroke matters, but the full meaning emerges only when the entire image is viewed together.

No single placement defines a person completely.

Instead, the chart reveals patterns that gradually unfold through life.

Some individuals discover their purpose early.

Others evolve through many different experiences before understanding their deeper calling.

The chart does not dictate the future.

It simply reveals the potential directions available to the soul.

Free Will and Conscious Choice

One of the greatest misunderstandings about astrology is the belief that it removes personal freedom.

In truth, the opposite is often the case.

Astrology increases awareness.

When individuals understand their tendencies, strengths, and challenges, they gain the ability to make more conscious decisions.

A person who recognizes a tendency toward impatience can learn patience.

Someone who struggles with fear can cultivate courage.

The birth chart does not remove choice.

It simply reveals the terrain through which the soul travels.

The Purpose of the Soul Map

Ultimately, the purpose of the birth chart is not prediction.

Its purpose is self-understanding.

When individuals understand themselves more deeply, they become better able to live in harmony with others and with the larger flow of life.

The chart becomes a mirror reflecting the deeper truths of the soul.

Through this reflection, life begins to feel less random and more meaningful.

The Chart as a Living Journey

Although the birth chart remains fixed, our relationship with it changes as we grow.

A placement that once felt difficult may later become a source of strength.

Challenges often transform into wisdom over time.

The chart is therefore not a static description of personality.

It is a living journey of awareness and transformation.

Each stage of life reveals new dimensions of its meaning.

The Invitation of Astrology

Astrology invites us to see life as part of a greater cosmic pattern.

It encourages reflection, curiosity, and compassion.

By understanding the patterns that shape our lives, we become more capable of navigating challenges and embracing opportunities.

The chart reminds us that every life has purpose.

Every soul carries a unique design.

And every journey contributes to the unfolding story of human existence.

CHAPTER 55: THE SOUL'S AWAKENING

Sleeper, Seeker, and the Awakened Soul

Every human being travels through stages of awareness.

Some move through life focused only on survival and daily responsibilities.

Others begin asking deeper questions about purpose, meaning, and truth.

Still others awaken to a profound understanding of their connection to all life.

These stages of development are part of the natural evolution of the soul.

Astrology can help illuminate this process by revealing the patterns and lessons that guide the soul's growth.

While every person's journey is unique, many spiritual traditions describe three primary stages of awakening.

These stages may be called many different things, but they can be understood simply as:

The Sleeper
The Seeker
The Awakened Soul

These stages are not labels meant to judge anyone.

They are simply reflections of the soul's current level of awareness in its unfolding journey.

The Sleeper

Living Within the Outer World

The Sleeper is a soul that is primarily focused on the physical world.

Life is experienced through daily responsibilities, survival needs, and external goals.

There is nothing wrong with this stage.

It is a natural and necessary part of human development.

During this stage, individuals often focus on:

- Career and financial stability
- Social identity
- Material achievement
- External validation
- Family responsibilities

The deeper spiritual questions of life may not yet feel urgent or important.

The individual may feel that life simply happens without deeper meaning beyond everyday events.

However, even within this stage, the soul is quietly learning.

Life experiences gradually plant seeds of curiosity that may later awaken deeper awareness.

The First Stirring

At some point, many individuals begin to feel a subtle inner restlessness.

Questions arise.

Why am I here?

What is the meaning of my life?

Is there something beyond what I can see?

These questions signal the beginning of the next stage.

The soul is beginning to awaken.

The Seeker

The Quest for Understanding

The Seeker is a soul that has begun actively searching for deeper truth.

During this stage, individuals may explore philosophy, spirituality, science, psychology, or personal growth.

The Seeker is driven by curiosity and a desire to understand the mysteries of existence.

Common experiences during this stage include:

- Exploring spiritual teachings
- Studying astrology or metaphysical systems
- Seeking mentors or teachers
- Questioning old beliefs
- Reflecting deeply on life experiences

The Seeker often realizes that the world is more complex and mysterious than previously understood.

Old assumptions may fall away.

New insights begin to emerge.

This stage can sometimes feel confusing because familiar beliefs are replaced by new perspectives.

However, this questioning is an essential part of spiritual growth.

The soul is learning to look beyond appearances and search for deeper truth.

The Awakening

As the Seeker continues exploring and reflecting, a profound shift may occur.

The individual begins to experience life from a broader perspective.

This marks the transition to the third stage.

The Awakened Soul

Living with Awareness

The Awakened Soul understands that life is interconnected.

Rather than seeing existence as random or chaotic, the awakened individual recognizes patterns, purpose, and unity.

This stage is often marked by qualities such as:

- Compassion for others
- Inner peace and acceptance
- A strong sense of purpose
- Awareness of spiritual connection
- Gratitude for life's experiences

The Awakened Soul no longer seeks external validation as the primary source of meaning.

Instead, fulfillment arises from alignment with deeper values and the desire to contribute positively to the world.

The awakened individual understands that growth continues throughout life.

Awakening is not a final destination.

It is an ongoing process of expanding awareness.

Astrology and Spiritual Growth

Astrology can serve as a powerful tool for those traveling through these stages.

For the Sleeper, astrology may initially appear as simple curiosity or entertainment.

For the Seeker, astrology becomes a system for understanding personality and life patterns.

For the Awakened Soul, astrology becomes something more profound, a reflection of the deeper harmony between human life and the cosmos.

It reveals that the universe is not random, but structured through patterns that mirror the journey of consciousness itself.

The Compassion of Awareness

One of the most important realizations of awakening is compassion.

When individuals understand that every soul is traveling its own path, judgment fades.

Some people are just beginning their journey.

Others are further along.

All are learning in their own time.

The awakened individual recognizes that every stage of development has value.

Each soul is unfolding according to its own rhythm.

The Endless Journey

Even awakening is not the final stage of the soul's development.

The universe continues expanding, and so does human awareness.

New insights, deeper compassion, and greater wisdom continue to emerge throughout life.

The soul's journey is not a straight line.

It is an ever-expanding spiral of discovery.

The Invitation

The purpose of spiritual awareness is not to escape the world.

It is to live within the world with greater clarity, kindness, and wisdom.

The awakened soul understands that every moment offers an opportunity for growth.

Every interaction becomes a chance to express compassion.

Every challenge becomes an opportunity for transformation.

The journey of awakening invites us to become more fully ourselves while recognizing our connection to all life.

CHAPTER 56:
LIVING YOUR SOUL MAP

Bringing Astrology Into Everyday Life

Understanding astrology is not meant to remain an intellectual exercise.

The true purpose of the Soul Map is to help us live more consciously, making choices that align with our deeper nature and purpose.

When we begin to understand the patterns within our birth chart, we gain insight into our strengths, our challenges, and the lessons our soul has chosen to explore.

But knowledge alone is not transformation.

Transformation occurs when awareness becomes action.

Living your Soul Map means allowing the wisdom of your chart to guide how you approach life's opportunities, relationships, and decisions.

Recognizing Your Strengths

Every birth chart contains natural gifts.

Some individuals possess strong creative abilities.

Others have a natural talent for leadership, communication, healing, or innovation.

These strengths are not accidents.

They are part of the soul's design.

When we recognize our strengths, we begin to understand how we can contribute meaningfully to the world.

Rather than comparing ourselves to others, we can focus on cultivating the unique qualities that make our journey special.

Each person carries a combination of abilities that no one else possesses in exactly the same way.

The Soul Map helps us discover those gifts.

Learning from Challenges

Just as every chart contains strengths, it also contains challenges.

Difficult aspects or placements may reveal areas where the soul must develop patience, resilience, or emotional awareness.

At first these challenges may appear as obstacles.

However, over time they often become the very experiences that shape our greatest wisdom.

A person who has faced hardship may develop deep compassion.

Someone who struggles with communication may eventually become an excellent teacher.

The birth chart reminds us that challenges are not punishments.

They are opportunities for growth.

The Importance of Self-Awareness

Self-awareness is one of the greatest gifts astrology offers.

When individuals become aware of their emotional patterns, motivations, and tendencies, they gain the ability to respond to life with greater wisdom.

Instead of reacting automatically, they can pause and choose how to act.

This awareness gradually leads to greater harmony in relationships, greater clarity in decision-making, and a deeper sense of inner peace.

The Soul Map becomes a mirror through which we can better understand ourselves.

Aligning with Your Purpose

One of the most meaningful insights astrology provides is the discovery of purpose.

Purpose does not necessarily mean fame, wealth, or public recognition.

Purpose simply means living in alignment with your authentic nature.

Some people fulfill their purpose through creativity.

Others through service, leadership, healing, teaching, or discovery.

Purpose is often revealed through the areas of life that bring the greatest sense of fulfillment and contribution.

When individuals align with their purpose, life begins to feel less like struggle and more like a natural unfolding.

Living in Harmony with the Cycles of Life

Astrology also reminds us that life moves in cycles.

Just as the seasons change, human life moves through periods of growth, challenge, reflection, and renewal.

Some periods bring expansion and opportunity.

Others invite patience and inner work.

Understanding these cycles can bring comfort during difficult times.

It reminds us that every stage of life has meaning.

No moment is wasted.

Every experience contributes to the soul's evolution.

Compassion for the Journey of Others

When we understand our own Soul Map, we also begin to recognize that every person is traveling their own unique path.

Some people are learning lessons about courage.

Others are exploring compassion.

Some are discovering creativity.

Others are developing wisdom through adversity.

When we see life through this lens, judgment becomes less important.

Compassion grows.

We begin to see humanity as a vast collection of souls, each contributing their own experience to the larger story of existence.

Living with Intention

Living your Soul Map ultimately means living with intention.

Rather than drifting through life unconsciously, you begin to make choices that reflect your values and aspirations.

You become more aware of how your actions affect others.

You begin to recognize the importance of kindness, patience, and understanding.

Each day becomes an opportunity to express the highest qualities of your soul.

The Soul Map as a Guide

Astrology does not remove uncertainty from life.

But it offers guidance.

It reminds us that life has patterns, rhythms, and meaning.

The Soul Map is not a set of rigid instructions.

It is a compass.

It points toward the deeper potential within each individual.

The journey itself is still ours to explore.

CHAPTER 57:
THE ETERNAL JOURNEY OF THE SOUL

A Closing Reflection

Every life is a story.

Some stories are quiet.

Others are dramatic and full of unexpected turns.

Yet beneath all these stories lies a deeper journey, the journey of the soul.

The soul enters the world with curiosity, courage, and a desire to experience life in all its forms.

Through joy and sorrow, success and struggle, it gathers wisdom.

The Soul Map described through astrology is simply a reflection of that journey.

It reminds us that our lives are part of a much larger cosmic pattern.

The Circle of Experience

The zodiac itself forms a circle.

This circle symbolizes the endless cycle of growth and renewal.

The soul moves through stages of identity, value, communication, emotion, creativity, service, partnership, transformation, wisdom, achievement, community, and spiritual awareness.

Each stage adds new understanding.

Each experience deepens the soul's awareness.

No stage is greater than another.

All are essential parts of the journey.

The Beauty of Human Life

Human life is both fragile and extraordinary.

Each person is given a limited amount of time to experience the world, to learn, to grow, and to share their gifts with others.

The beauty of life does not lie in perfection.

It lies in the courage to grow, to love, and to seek understanding.

Every act of kindness, every moment of courage, and every effort to learn brings the soul closer to its highest potential.

The Mystery of the Universe

Despite all that we discover through science, philosophy, and spirituality, the universe still holds profound mystery.

Astrology offers one way of exploring that mystery.

It reminds us that human life is connected to the rhythms of the cosmos.

The same forces that guide the movement of stars and planets also influence the patterns of human experience.

This connection invites humility and wonder.

It encourages us to see ourselves not as separate from the universe, but as part of its unfolding story.

The Legacy We Leave

In the end, the most meaningful legacy we leave is not measured by wealth or recognition.

It is measured by the lives we touch.

The kindness we show.

The wisdom we share.

The love we give.

These are the true contributions that ripple outward through time.

Long after our individual journey ends, the effects of our actions continue influencing the lives of others.

The Soul's Continuing Journey

The journey of the soul does not end with a single lifetime.

Many spiritual traditions suggest that consciousness continues evolving beyond the boundaries of one life.

Whether through memory, legacy, or spiritual continuation, the essence of the soul carries forward.

Every experience contributes to the growth of awareness.

Every life adds another chapter to the soul's story.

A Final Reflection

If there is one message that emerges from the study of astrology and the journey of the soul, it is this:

Life has meaning.

Each person carries within them a unique combination of gifts, lessons, and potential.

When individuals begin to understand themselves more deeply, they gain the ability to live with greater wisdom, compassion, and purpose.

The Soul Map is not a destination.

It is an invitation.

An invitation to explore the mysteries of existence.

An invitation to grow.

An invitation to become the fullest expression of the soul you were meant to be.

The Journey Continues

As you close this book, remember that your journey is still unfolding.

New experiences await.

New insights will emerge.

New opportunities for growth will appear.

The stars continue moving.

The universe continues expanding.

And the soul continues its timeless journey of discovery.

May your path be filled with curiosity, courage, wisdom, and compassion.

And may the map of the heavens always remind you that you are part of something vast, beautiful, and eternal.

ABOUT THE AUTHOR

Tina Ketch is an accomplished author, spiritual explorer, and lifelong student of the mysteries of life. With more than sixty books to her name, her work explores themes of personal transformation, astrology, vibrational energy, emotional healing, and the deeper journey of the human soul.

Drawing from decades of study in astrology, religion, psychology, and spiritual philosophy, Tina offers readers a thoughtful and compassionate perspective on life's most profound questions. Her writing invites readers to look beyond ordinary experience and discover the deeper patterns that shape purpose, growth, and awakening.

Tina's life has been marked by both extraordinary spiritual exploration and deep personal insight. Her experiences, including years of meditation and research in a pyramid she had built in Florida, have inspired her to explore the connection between cosmic forces, consciousness, and human destiny.

Today, Tina continues to write, teach, and share her insights with readers around the world. Through her books, she encourages others to explore their own inner wisdom, understand the rhythms of the universe, and live with greater awareness, compassion, and purpose.

Learn more about her work at TinaKetch.com.

www.ingramcontent.com/pod-product-compliance
Lightning Source LLC
LaVergne TN
LVHW020653110826
845149LV00012B/1978